Landscapes of
TUSCANY

a countryside guide

Elizabeth Mizon

SUNFLOWER BOOKS

For Judith, the Little Sisters and my Florentine friends

First published 2000
by Sunflower Books™
12 Kendrick Mews
London SW7 3HG, UK

ISBN 1-85691-155-1

Waymarked tabernacle

Important note to the reader

We have tried to ensure that the descriptions and maps in this book are error-free at press date. The book will be updated, where necessary, whenever future printings permit. It will be very helpful for us to receive your comments (sent in care of the publishers, please) for the updating of future printings.

   We also rely on those who use this book — especially walkers — to take along a good supply of common sense when they explore. Conditions change fairly rapidly in Tuscany, and *storm damage or bulldozing may make a route unsafe at any time*. If the route is not as we outline it here, and your way ahead is not secure, return to the point of departure. *Never attempt to complete a tour or walk under hazardous conditions!* Please read carefully the notes on pages 40-41 and 137-141, as well as the introductory comments at the beginning of each tour and walk (regarding road conditions, equipment, grade, distances and time, etc). Explore *safely*, while at the same time respecting the beauty of the countryside.

Cover: River Arno at Castel San Niccolò (Car tour 4)
Title page: poppy fields in the Mugello (Car tour 1)
Above: waymarked tabernacle on the short walk at Castelfranco (Car tour 4)

Photographs: the author
Maps: Pat Underwood and Polly Senior Cartography, based on the 1:25 000 maps of the Istituto Geografico Militare and the Carta dei Sentieri e Rifugi (see page 40)
A CIP catalogue record for this book is available from the British Library.
Printed and bound in England: Brightsea Press, Exeter

10 9 8 7 6 5 4 3 2 1

Contents

4 Landscapes of Tuscany

Preface

Before we lived near Florence, we had a vague idea that Tuscany and the 'Chianti' area were almost synonymous. How wrong we were.

From Florence we discovered the richness of the countryside that could be reached on foot even from the centre of the city. The richness comes from the unique history of the area; not only from the influence of the nobility with their wars and battles, and later from their love of art and culture, but from the peasants, whose labours have shaped the hillsides, built the tracks and the tiny wayside chapels.

Recent history has also left its mark. After the two world wars, farming families abandoned the countryside for apartments in the towns. The countryside was left almost free to return to nature. And nature returned abundant, providing natural rock gardens of *Cistus* and miniature evergreens. Wild flowers painted the floor of the olive groves yellow and white in late spring. Wild blue irises and vivid red poppies decorated the dry stone walls. Butterflies, bright green lizards, and silent animals completed the picture.

Although the farmhouses are once more being lived in, much of that richness remains, as does the myriad of paths and tracks that link one tiny hamlet with another through this free-range landscape.

And this we found just around Florence. From there we explored further and realised that richness is a feature of the whole of Tuscany. There is such a variety of beautiful countryside. Within Tuscany's boundaries are set, side by side, an array of landscapes so diverse it is as if a geography teacher had set it up as a sampler. To the north and east are the high mountains of the Apennines, steep and austere as any mountain barrier. Sub-Apennine ranges are enclosed within, the most distinctive of which is the Alpi Apuane. These mountains are more like the Dolomites in structure, are on the west coast and are famous for providing Italy with much of its marble.

There are of course the rolling hills of the Chianti, so photogenic with their lines of vines, hilltop villages and cypress trees. Further south the hills become more gently curved and sensuous, but divided by strange, deeply-eroded ravines. This is the Sienese Crete, which stretches almost to the slopes of Monte Amiata, an extinct volcano, now a ski resort. Surrounding the volcano is land rich in minerals and hot springs. What better than a therapeutic bath after a long walk? Flat coastal plains, deep limestone canyons, lush river valleys; Tuscany has so much — and all bathed in walker-friendly weather and decorated by some of the world's best architects and landscape architects.

Whether you explore by car or on foot, Tuscany needs time. There is so much to see, so many surprises waiting for you. Whether it is discovering a minute hamlet of old houses with bright red geraniums tucked into every sort of pot, or wild flowers that you know only as garden flowers, or a porcupine quill lying on the path, it needs time. Stand and stare; let the beauty and the history and the friendly people seep into your soul. Do half of what you intended, then come back another time to see some more.

Acknowledgements

I could never have had the adventure of preparing this book without the support and companionship of my husband Grayham. He was infinitely willing to join me on trips, even after a week of his own work, and infinitely patient as we tried different routes.

Thanks, too, to all my friends from all over the world who accompanied me exploring these memorable hills. They made this task even more wonderful.

Useful books

For the historical background to man-made monuments I enjoy the *Cadogan Guide to Tuscany and Umbria*, whereas *Wild Italy* (Sheldrake Press) has good material on wild life and nature throughout Italy.

GLOSSARY

agriturismo — farms providing holiday accommodation; see photograph pages 34-35 and 'Where to stay', page 137

balze — cliffs, crags; see photograph page 86

bivio — fork, junction

bosco — woodland

buca — cave, hole

burraia — cold store; see article page 106

callare — pass

capanna — hut

cava — quarry; see article on page 65

cima — summit

col/colle — pass

collina — hill

contadino — peasant

costa, cresta — ridge

est — east

fattora, fattoria — see articles on pages 57, 105, 129

foce — pass, shoulder or mouth

fiume — river

frana — landslide

grotta — cave

lago — lake

marginetta — sacred stone shelter; see article on page 121

marmo — marble

mezzadria — crop-sharing; see articles on pages 57 and 105

montagna — mountain

monte — mount

mulattiera — mule track

nebbia — fog, mist

nord — north

passo — pass

pietra serena —

'serene stone'; see articles on pages 47 and 65

pizzo — peak

poggio — hillock, knoll

ponte — bridge

ovest — west

rifugio — mountain hut/refuge providing accommodation for hikers

rocca — ruined castle

sella — saddle

sentiero — path, trail

sorgente — spring

sud — south

tabernacolo — shrine; see article on page 121

torrente — stream

valle — valley

via ferrata — steep route with fixed steel cable

❀ Getting about

Unless you are the sort of person who really enjoys delving into train and bus timetables and conquering their mysteries, the answer to getting about in Tuscany must be the **car**. Bringing your own car to Italy is eminently feasible; indeed I have always enjoyed the 14-hour drive from the Channel ports, when we have taken two days for the drive. Motor-rail is perhaps a more relaxing alternative. Hire cars are readily available at all airports, but can be much less expensive if you organise the hire car before you arrive in Italy.

Trains are reasonably reliable and inexpensive for those lucky enough to have a destination that happens to be on a train line.

Taxis are expensive, so be sure to get a quote before you start your journey.

The most comprehensive form of public transport is the **bus**. There are regular inter-city services and services to small towns and villages. These latter, however, are designed to get villagers into town to work, not walkers into villages in the morning. Services are very scarce at weekends. Tuscany is served by several bus companies, details of which you can find on page 140. Many bus companies run special whole or part-day sightseeing coach trips. Details of these and timetables for the local buses are available from bus stations and some tourist offices.

Many of the walks in this book are accessible by public transport, and under 'How to get there' I tell you which company operates the route and the journey time. On pages 140-141 there is more information about buses. If you do intend to rely on public transport, then I recommend you stay in a city which is a transport hub. Florence and Siena especially are well served. You will also need to spend some time planning, and be good at time-keeping.

Generally the buses are reliable and comfortable, but getting timetable information by telephone can be very difficult; it is best to visit the bus stations. In rural areas, local buses supplement those of the companies listed on page 140. This means that the bus you are expecting may have a different name on the side.

All the walks are on or near car tours. Either follow the tour itself, or use the touring map for a more direct route. Almost all the walks are circular. If the walk is linear, there will be convenient buses to get you to the start or back.

❋ Picnicking

When Italians eat in the countryside it is usually at a restaurant with a good view and a large car park, or they set up a dining area near their car, with table, chairs, and tablecloth. They are often escaping the city heat. Official picnic areas with tables are quite rare in Tuscany, but places to picnic are not. Pick your spot among the acres of unfenced, uncultivated land. All you need is something to sit on, like a car rug! As Tuscany is so wooded, it is rare that there isn't a tree to provide a little shade. Just leave no trace of your having been there, especially as landowners are very tolerant of tidy picnickers. Below I suggest a few picnic places where you might either swim or take a short walk.

1 FLORENCE

5-10min on foot. ATAF 🚌 or 🚐 to Piazzale Michelangiolo in Florence. From the Piazzale cross the road and walk up Viale Galilei for one minute. Turn left on Via San Miniato Monte (between the churches), then go right on Via del Giramonte, where you will find a stand of cypresses behind the church and cemetery of San Miniato. This grassy shady spot, with a fine view, is ideal if you are visiting the city and would like a quiet spot to eat your sandwiches.

2 MONTE PRATONE (map pages 42-43)

25min on foot. Access by 🚐: from Fiesole (the 8km-point in Car tour 1) follow signs for Olmo. About 2km further on, turn right for Monte Fanna. When this road turns left about 2km uphill, park a short way along on

he left, by a red and white bar-gate. Follow the track (CAI 2) past two
ed and white barriers, up to the receiving station at Monte Fanna. From
here the track continues 5min more to Monte Pratone, a wide meadow
with fine views. It is a wonderful spot on a summer evening, especially
when you walk back towards the lights of Florence in the valley.

3 MONTE SENARIO (map page 42-43; nearby photograph overleaf)

up to 10min on foot. SITA 🚌 or 🚗 to Monte Senario (the 22km-point
in Car tour 1); park before the church. Walk back down the road to the
large gate by a cross. Go through the gate to the ridge path, with plenty
of picnic spots (but the best views are near the gate). If you go as far as
a small meadow, you will find shade. Near the monastery there are
many short walks to hermitages (and the ice house shown on page 45).

4 GIOGO DI SCARPERIA (map pages 60-61) 🅿

20-30min on foot. SITA 🚌 or 🚗 to the Giogo Pass in the Mugello (38km
from Florence; the 56km-point in Car tour 1). Alight or park at the pass.
From here you can follow the red and white waymarks of the CAI 00 to
the east or northwest. Either walk east along the ridge track across from
the bar, to find shaded picnic tables on the left and panoramic views of
the Apennines (20min). Or follow the footpath a little way uphill from
the bar, to the northwest (a climb of 150m/500ft; 30min): you will reach
a spectacular ridge with views southwest over the Mugello and its
horseshoe of mountains, and northeast to Firenzola set in a ring of peaks.
There are many picnic spots in the meadow here.

5 CAMAGGIORE (touring map; see photograph page 10)

5min on foot. Access by 🚗: follow Car tour 1 past Firenzuola (the 67km-
point). After the road crosses to the eastern bank of the river, turn left
downhill to Camaggiore (at 74km). Park up by the church. You can
picnic or swim by the bridge and, as the CAI 729 passes by the church,
there are ample opportunities for a stroll.

6 LA PANCA (map page 91) 🅿

10-15min on foot. Access by 🚗: park in the hamlet of La Panca (the
32km-point on Car tour 2). There are two suggestions
here. Either take the road climbing at 90° off the main
road, across from the only restaurant; this is the
waymarked CAI 00. Just beyond the houses, take the
CAI 18 track off to the right, to a pretty clearing where
a lean-to covers a long rickety table and seats (10min;
no view). If you prefer less space but a view, don't take
CAI 18 beyond the houses, but continue up the CAI 00,
alongside the green fence. After 10min you will reach
a sunny bank with a view over the Chianti hills.

7 PARCO DI MONTE SAN MICHELE (touring map)

20min on foot. Access by 🚗: park at the road junction
as soon as you reach the ridge of Monte San Michele
(the 41km-point in Car tour 2). Walk to the right along
the track, and up the path on the right to the large cross
on Monte Domini. View over the Arno Valley and the
Alpe di San Benedetto in the Apennines. For a shady

*Reservoir at Vetta le Croci, a favourite spot for Italians
to picnic on Sunday afternoons (Car tour 1, Walk 1)*

Left: Monte Senario (near Picnic 3); right: river at Camaggiore (top; Picnic 5) and Vitozza's caves (Picnic 19)

site, continue by car: turn left at the ridge and follow the signs for the hotel (43km), where there is a large picnic area.

8 PASQUILIO PASS (touring map)

5-10min on foot. Access by 🚗: park at Pasquilio Pass. After San Carlo (the 7km-point on Car tour 3) and Pariana, take the next right turn (this turn is so sharp that you must first carry on a short distance to a lay-by where you can make a U-turn). Some 6km along, the road ends at the Pasquilio Pass, where there is a track to a hotel and a WW2 monument. Walk up some steps, then take the path past the statue of Enrico Pea. This becomes a lovely ridge path on the slopes of Monte Belvedere, with good picnic spots.

9 ISOLA SANTA (touring map) 🛆

5min on foot. Access by 🚗: park in the lay-by above Isola Santa (13km from Castelnuovo; the 32km-point on Car tour 3). Walk down the road for two minutes, then go through a gap in the wall on the right, to a deserted village. Between the church and the lake you will find a stone hut with picnic tables; it is used by fishermen, but if they are not there, do take advantage of it. Or picnic on the grassy banks by the shore of the lake. For a short walk, follow the CAI 9 across the dam wall and turn right in front of a house. At a fork, follow the lower path for a short while, above the lake. You are at the heart of the Alpi Apuane here.

10 BELOW MONTE FALCO (map pages 78-79) 🛆

30min on foot. Access by 🚗: see Walk 10, page 97, and park at the Passo la Calla in the Alpe di San Benedetto (15km above Stia, reached from the 48km-point on Car tour 4). There are picnic tables at the pass but, if you prefer a walk, follow the CAI 00 path on the left, up through delightful beech woods, towards Monte Falco. After about 30min climbing you come to a grassy clearing with lovely views.

11 ODINA (map pages 84-85)

17min on foot. Access by 🚗: see Short walk 12-1 on page 83, to park near Odina (18km from the Valdarno exit on the A1 autostrada; Car tour 4). Follow Short walk 12-1, taking the CAI 33 track as far as the green gate-posts. Turn right on the grassy track here, quickly coming to a wide terrace with a wonderful view and woody places for children to explore.

12 MONTAUTO (map page 104)

20min on foot. Access by 🚗: from San Gimignano (the 21km-point on Car tour 5) follow the road signposted to Volterra. 1km downhill, turn left towards Montauto. At the T-junction just below Montauto, turn left and park. Walk back to the junction and take the first lane on the left. This leads up to a ridge where you turn right on a track signposted to Ciuciano. Five minutes along, the woods open up to reveal fine views, and there are plenty of grassy spots to picnic.

13 POGGIO DI VAIANO (touring map)

5-10min on foot. Access by 🚗: following Car tour 5, park about 15km beyond San Gimignano (1km past the signs for La Striscia on the right). Follow the track on the left, behind the barrier; it heads along the ridge, affording fine views. The area is scrub of pines, heather and oaks.

14 CHIUSURE (map page 113)

20min on foot. Access by 🚗: park just outside Chiusure (the 39km-point on Car tour 6). Just before the road from Monte Oliveto turns sharp left to encircle the village, take the unsealed road descending to the right. It runs along a ridge surrounded by canyons, opposite the monastery. The best picnic spot is just past a house, in a meadow with good views.

15 SANT'ANNA (touring map) 🏕

15min on foot. Access by 🚗: park 2km after leaving Caselmuzio on the Pienza road, where there are shaded picnic tables (11km from Pienza; the 59km-point on Car tour 6). Afterwards, follow the pleasant cypress-lined track to the old monastery of Sant'Anna, used as the setting for much of the film 'The English Patient'.

16 SANT'ANTIMO (map page 115; photographs page 116)

5-20min on foot. TRA-IN 🚌 or 🚗 to Sant'Antimo (10km from Montalcino; the 19km-point on Car tour 7). From the car park or bus stop, walk towards the church, but continue on the track straight ahead instead of turning left. Follow the track to the left (do not cross the stream). In 5min you come to a small grassy area, just right for a quiet lunch.

17 VIVO D'ORCIA (map page 127; photographs page 128) 🏕

10-30min on foot. Access by 🚗: park as for Walk 24, page 126 (the 71km-point on Car tour 7). Follow Walk 24 for 10min, to a couple of picnic tables by a very pleasant waterfall. Or continue for 20min more, to picnic tables in a wood, near a spring and the chapel of Ermicciolo.

18 FIORA RIVER (touring map)

up to 5min on foot. Access by 🚗: park by the bridge over the River Fiora, on the road between Sovana and Semproniano (9km from Pitigliano; the 46km-point on Car tour 8). Looking upstream, take the track to the right of the river. It leads to the river bed (where the best views are looking upstream). We enjoyed a refreshing swim here.

19 VITOZZA (touring map; photograph opposite, bottom right) 🏕

20min on foot. Access by 🚗: park in the village of San Quirico (the 110km-point on Car tour 8), or in Vitozza's signposted car park (see Car tour 8, page 39). Follow the signs to the cave dwellings (small entrance charge). There are a few picnic tables and many interesting picnic spots among the trees.

Touring

In choosing these tours my intention has been to provide an overview of Tuscany's varied and beautiful landscapes. All of these areas are also perfect for out-of-doors activities such as hiking, biking, horse-riding and picnicking.

The tours are largely devoted to the countryside, although many do visit famous towns and villages. The historical and artistic treasures of Tuscany are discussed in standard guide-books, and information is available from tourist offices. The addresses and telephone numbers of relevant **tourist offices** are given at the top of each tour, but bear in mind that it is not always easy to make contact by telephone (Saturday morning is the best time). English is usually spoken at the tourist offices. Remember they, like everyone else in Tuscany, will be closed between 13.00-15.00 (or 16.00) for the long lunch break, opening again until about 19.30.

The tours are either circular or start and finish on motor-way access points. Join the circuit where convenient. All the tours *can* be done in a day, although you may prefer to take longer. Where possible, I have indicated where the tours can be shortened. Don't expect to average more than **20mph/35kmh**, especially on mountain roads. *Drive carefully!*

The **touring maps** inside the back cover (scale 1:400,000) are designed to be held out opposite the touring notes and

contain a **key to the symbols** in the touring notes. If you wish to buy another map for touring, I recommend the 1:200,000 'Toscana' map published by the Touring Club Italiano.

Petrol stations are found usually only in towns and villages and are often closed on Sundays. *Do fill up before you set off.* Motorway services are open 24h. **Bars** are really important in Italy — not only for a great coffee, but for toilets, bus tickets, and general information.

Signposting in Tuscany is very reliable so, rather than give complicated directions, I have just indicated the signposting. Parking areas in towns are also well marked. **Road numbers** are variously prefixed by SS *(strada statale)*, SP *(strada provinciale)*, or N *(numero)*, but you need only note the *number*. The **road signs** are international, but always keep in mind the following important **motoring laws**.

- **Vehicles coming from the right have priority**, unless the road markings indicate otherwise. Take special care at roundabouts, especially if priority is to the right.
- **Unbroken lines** in the centre of the road must not be crossed.
- **At a junction with traffic lights**, pedestrians can be crossing the road with a green light, while cars have a green light to turn right or left. The **pedestrians have priority**.
- **Motorway signposting** is green; main roads are signposted in blue.
- Always carry all your **documents** with you when you drive: passport, licence, car registration document, insurance certificate and 'Green Card' (the latter not essential, but advisable).

Opening hours can be very erratic. If you find something that you want to see is open, sieze the opportunity!

Pitigliano (Car tour 8; Walk 25) from Madonna delle Grazie Church

1 THE FOOTHILLS OF THE APENNINES — THE MUGELLO

Florence • Fiesole • Bivigliano • Vaglia • San Piero a Sieve • Scarperia • Giogo di Scarperia • Firenzuola • Palazzuolo sul Senio • Passo Sambuca • Borgo San Lorenzo • Florence

146km/90mi; 4h driving

On route: Picnics (see **P** symbol and pages 8-11) 1-5; Walks 1-5

This day-trip into the mountains to the north of Florence takes you from the flat valley of the Arno up to the Sambuca Pass. Inevitably, in this mountainous area the winding roads demand concentration, but they are generally well maintained and afford some spectacular alpine views. If you are in Tuscany in high summer, this is a particularly good drive, as the air cools mercifully on the climb and you pass a river perfect for an icy dip. The far point of the drive is the village of Palazzuolo, one of the finalists in the 'Ideal Village' competition for the whole of Italy.

Opening hours, information offices (*i*), and market days (⌑)
Fiesole: *i* at Piazza Mino 37, mornings only; tel: 055 598720; ⌑ Sat
Borgo San Lorenzo: *i* (for the Mugello region) at Via Bandini 6, part-time; tel: 055 8458793; ⌑ Tue
Palazzuolo: *i* at Piazza E Alpi 1, tel: 055 8046125; ⌑ Sat; Museum (of peasant life; small entrance fee payable) open Sun/holidays from 15.00-18.00 (16.00-19.00 in July and Aug)

From Florence take the well-signposted road to Fiesole, attractive all year round, with its coloured villas perching on the hillside, but particularly stunning in April, when the wisteria and lilac are in blossom. There is much to see in **Fiesole★** (8km/5mi ✝⛪△✗🚉📷🚍M). Parking is in the main square, near the tourist office (Piazza Mino, photograph page 50). If you have time for just one of Fiesole's sights, find Via di San Francesco by the front of the cathedral and take a five-minute walk up to the beautiful old church of San Francesco, with monks' cells and a dramatic view of Florence.

Continue up through the village, following signs for Olmo (you pass the turn-off right for Monte Fanna and Monte Pratone after 2km; **P**2). The road winds above the Mugnone River through typical Florentine countryside — olive groves, farmhouses and villas. Go straight over two crossroads. There is a field and a reservoir on the right at the second crossroad, **Vetta le Croci** (17km/11mi ✗🚍), where city-dwellers love to picnic on Sunday afternoons (photographs pages 8-9 and opposite).

Now follow signs to Vaglia. At the next major junction turn right towards the monastery of Monte Senario. This ridge road is one of my favourites, with its panorama towards the endless grey-blue mountain horizons where the tour is heading. The monastery rises straight ahead. As you follow the signs for the monastery, stop at a parking area with a huge wooden cross, to visit the ice house shown on page 45. It is just down the rough track from the top end of the car park. You can also walk to the monastery from here, up through

Top: wisteria and church of San Francesco at Fiesole (left and middle); view towards Monte Giovi from Vetta le Croci (right). Left: the 16th-century Fortezza di San Martino, built by the Medicis to guard Florence from the north. It was never used in battle and has been converted into a rather eccentric private house, not open to the public.

the gate-posts leading from the track into dark pines. Continuing by car, the asphalt takes you almost all the way up to the church. Leave your car in the car park and enjoy the serenity of this holy place. The church land around **Monte Senario** (22km/15mi ✝☞☎🅿3; Walk 1; history page 44) is a maze of paths to grottoes, cells and viewing areas.

When you leave the monastery, take the same road back down the hill initially, but then turn right to **Bivigliano** (24km/15mi ▲▲△✕🅿🚌), where Walk 1 begins. The road curves between the (mainly holiday) homes of the village to the main street. Turn right here and, still following the Vaglia signs, follow the hairpins down into the valley and the main Florence/Mugello road (SS65). Here in **Vaglia** (29km/18mi 🅿🚌🔭) you meet the recently-reopened railway line, probably one of just a very few new railways in Europe. Just before you turn right to join the SS65 and the railway, there is a picnic area on the bank of the River Carza (🔭).

Turn right on the main road, eventually coming to a roundabout (35km), where a left turn leads to the *autostrada* and Bologna. Take the second right off the roundabout, into the centre of **San Piero** (37km/23mi ✝🍴▲▲△✕🅿🚌; Walk 4). Access to the fortress shown above is via a rough narrow road signposted up to the left, but I suggest you walk and then stroll outside the castle's 1600m-long walls.

Leave San Piero on the road signposted to Scarperia, crossing the River Sieve. Take the second road to the left, but then turn right following the signs to Gabbiano and the golf course. This is the prettiest, yet most unassuming of roads. It links all the farms sitting on the ridge, the whole in a basin surrounded by the dramatic Apennines. (The road is poorly surfaced, so take your time; there will probably be no traffic behind you.) After an unsealed stretch, when the road ends, turn right to **Sant'Agata** (42.5km/27mi ✝🚌M; Walk 5), another gem of a hamlet with an important and beautiful 12th-century church.

Now you are heading down towards Scarperia. Just before Scarperia*, take the bypass for Firenzuola and Imola. Continue towards Firenzuola via the **Giogo** (Yoke) **di Scarperia**, a pass at 882m/2893ft (56km/35mi ✕🍴🛏️🚻⛺🅿4). A stop is a must if you are a peak-freak like me. The Apennines ridge walk CAI 00 crosses here (Alternative walk 5).

The road to Firenzuola curves down the valley with broad views over a varied landscape of alpine meadows and forests enclosed by the peaks of the northern Apennines. **Firenzuola** (67km/42mi 🛏️🏨△✕🚻🛏️) is a working town that had to be rebuilt after the war. The old street plan was retained, giving the place a friendly feel. Leave Firenzuola in the direction of Imola. The road is bordered by great cliffs of stone, shaped by quarrying of *pietra serena*. Now the road meanders parallel with the river, which flows through the gorge below. Watch for the dramatic rock strata and rope bridge at **San Pellegrino**. The bridge goes from the village to an allotment garden, but I would have to be very hungry before I would pick the lettuces there! After crossing the river, 'Camaggiore' is marked to the left (74km/46mi). If you are hot and sticky, turn left here, cross the bridge, park up at the church and head for the river — a popular swimming and picnicking spot (*P*5; photograph page 10). Otherwise take the next right for Palazzuolo, up and over the watershed with flowering meadows and far-reaching views. **Palazzuolo★** (95km/58mi 👣△✕🚻🛏️M) is an attractive village, with a river in the centre, parks, and old stone houses clustered along the hillside.

To end the tour, retrace your route to the edge of Palazzuolo, but then go left (signposted to Florence) on the N447 that climbs over the Alpe di San Benedetto via the **Passo Sambuca** (1061m/3480ft). This alpine road joins the road from Marradi at the **Col dell'Alpe** (110km/68mi). Go right here and, in the centre of **Borgo San Lorenzo★** (118km/73mi 👣🏨✕🚻🛏️), where Florence is signposted two ways, keep left via the 'Faentina'. Back at **Olmo**, turn right to round the top of the valley. Join the SS65 at **Pratolino**, where the Parco Demidoff is open to the public in summer. Keep left on the main road, the Via Bolognese, back to **Florence** (146km). (From Pian di San Bartolo, 9km short of Florence, a road signposted right to Cercina gives access to Walk 3).

*Scarperia★ (46km/29mi 👣🏨✕🚻🛏️M) is famous today for making knives, an industry that developed from swords and armour production in the past. The notable Palazzo Vicari, now the town hall, was built in 1306, but has been modified over the centuries, partly as a result of earthquake damage. The exterior is covered with stone coats of arms of the local families, almost like sticking plaster keeping the place together.

2 HILLTOP VILLAGES AND GENTLE HILLS OF THE CHIANTI

Florence • Impruneta • Strada in Chianti • Dudda • Parco San Michele • Radda in Chianti • Castellina in Chianti • Panzano • Montefioralle • Greve in Chianti • Grassina • Florence

111km/69mi; 3h30min driving

En route: Picnics (see *P* symbol and pages 8-11) 1, 6, 7; Walks 13-17

Chianti comprises the geographical area between Florence and Siena bounded now by two major roads, the superstrada *to the west and the A1* autostrada *to the east. Historically it was the territory of the Lega del Chianti, protected by local barons. In 1716 the Grand Duke of Tuscany proclaimed in a legal document that only wine from this area could be called Chianti — the first wine to have its name protected in this way. The tour starts in Florence, but you can join the circuit wherever is convenient: the most northerly point of the circuit is Impruneta and the most southerly Castellina. The tour is a very gentle run around the northwest corner of the Chianti, along quiet roads looking out to wooded hills, vineyards and stone farmhouses. Although the tour is lovely in any season, May is the perfect month, as the roadsides are an artist's palette of reds and yellows. Along the way there are* fattorias *offering wine-tastings, as well as stone villages where the buildings are pushed together into the tiniest space, making them a joy to explore.*

Opening hours, information offices (*i*), and market days (⚖)
Impruneta: *i* at Via G. Mazzini 1; tel: 055 2313729; ⚖ Sat
Radda: *i* at Piazza Ferrucci 1, part-time only; tel: 0577 738494; ⚖ 4th Mon of every month
Greve: *i* at Via Luca Cini, closed in winter; tel: 055 85451; ⚖ Sat
Castellina: *i* at Via della Rocca 12; tel: 0577 740620; ⚖ Sat

Leave Florence in grand style from the Piazzale Michelangiolo (*P*1), driving up and along Viale Galileo Galilei with its refreshing space, manicured gardens and evergreens. On the slope down towards Porto Romano, take the road to the left signposted to Siena and the Poggio Imperiale. Beyond the sculptured umbrella pines, at the traffic lights, turn left towards the imposing Poggio Imperiale. Turn right at the *palazzo,* down towards Galluzzo. This old road ends at a mini-roundabout, where you go left, following signs for Impruneta. You are soon out of the city, with the rolling hills of the Chianti ahead of you and the olive-tree landscape of rural Florence on all sides. Climbing gently to the villages of **Pozzolatico** and **Mezzomonte**, you enjoy long panoramas of the Arno Valley with its surrounding circle of mountains.

You should be able to park in the large square at **Impruneta★** (16km/10mi ✝⛰△✕🚐🅿M) if it is not market day. Visit the information office and collect directions to the famous ceramic works shown overleaf; visit the magnificent church and museum of Santa Maria too. Then take the road at the left of the church, the SP69 to Strada in Chianti. Follow this cypress-lined road, watching out for a series of tabernacles that punctuate the first stretch. They lead off to the

17

Left: medieval covered street in Castellina; right terracotta yard in Impruneta

right, to the cemetery on the hill (📷). Cruise down to the junction with the SS222 and turn right, through **Strada** (20km/12mi ✕🍴🛒). This road is called the 'Chiantigana'. Watch for your next turn-off (at 23km): go left towards Figline and Cintoia. This is a delightfully-winding and wooded road, with occasional views across to hills, some crowned with houses. **Mugnana** (26km/16mi; Walk 14), with its medieval castle and 60m/200ft-high tower, is followed by **Cintoia** (28km/17mi 🛈), best known locally as a source of bottled water, but with a 7th-century parish church worth a visit.

The route is now climbing into the 'Mountains of the Chianti', although hills would be a more accurate description. At **La Panca** (32km/20mi ✕🛒), the wonderful CAI 00 (**P**6) Florence to Siena walk crosses the valley. The view opens out here, with vineyards in the foreground — so disciplined in their neat rows, yet so evocative.

This road ends at a T-junction (35km/22mi): turn left towards Figline, through village of **Dudda** with its pretty roadside church. Turn right after the factory and, just beyond **Lucolena** (🛈🏨🛌✕) and **Dunezzano**, turn sharp right (40km), following signs for Monte San Michele and Greve). At the end of the climb you meet an unsealed road along the wide, airy, peaceful ridge (41km). The road to the right leads to a viewpoint with a huge and rather ugly cross (a first setting for **P**7), then it descends all the way to Greve. (If time has flown you can pick up the tour towards its end in Greve.) To the left of the junction the road leads to the **Parco di Monte San Michele** (43km 🛌✕📷🛒**P**7), a picnic site. In fact this whole unspoiled area is full of places to picnic or stroll.

The route off the ridge is back the way you came. At the junction for Lucolena, turn right. About 2km further along, you can park on the left for Walk 16 (48km/30mi 📷), at the junction of two paths — the CAI 9 and CAI 00. From here it's a climb of 1.5km up the CAI 00 to the summit of Monte San Michele, at 892m/2925ft the top of the Chianti Mountains.

Leaving the tops, you are now heading down towards Radda in Chianti along a road which is unsealed for a short way. As you descend, waves of hills — the essence of the Chianti landscape — will fill your view. Continue past the entrance to the hilltop hamlet of Badiaccia, which was once an important monastery. (If you would like to explore the Parco di Cavriglia★ (🏔🍴🍷🎋), with its trails, animals, and other exhibits, follow the signs to the left.) Then drive down past the **Fattoria d'Albola** (🏰); its castle dates from 1000 to 1300. This *fattoria* is now a well-known winery with a tasting room (open weekdays only). If no one sees you, knock at the office door and someone will escort you to the tasting room.

The next stretch of road descends through vineyards, home of the wines you may just have been tasting. It is one of my favourite roads in Chianti, as the surrounding fields are so patterned and orderly, yet natural and calm — beautiful in every season (photograph pages 102-103). At a junction (58km), go left for Gaiole if you want to park for Walk 15, or follow signs for Greve and then Volpaia, if you are doing Walk 16 from Volpaia. Otherwise continue straight on to **Radda**★ (60km/37mi 🚻🏔🍴🍷🍷). This pretty village caters well for tourists and has interesting medieval covered corridors worth exploring.

Leaving Radda, take the SS429 towards Castellina. From this road the wooded nature of much of Chianti is very obvious. Large stretches of the land are uncultivated, left to oak trees and junipers, rock roses, broom and wild flowers. **Castellina**★ (70km/43.5mi 🏰🏔🍴🍷🍷M) is thought by some to be one of the most important and most charming villages of this wine-growing area. It boasts a *rocca* (citadel) and a medieval covered street (see opposite), as well as plenty of places to taste wine.

From Castellina the tour heads back to Florence. Take the Radda road again, but then turn off left for Panzano and Greve. Watch carefully for a left turn signposted to San Casciano and Mercatale. Follow these signs through **Panzano** (83km/51.5mi 🚻🍴🍷) and on towards the summit of Monte Calvario, with views over the Greve Valley. This really *is* the heart of the Chianti Classico wine-growing region. Beyond the summit, you could continue ahead to the signposted left turn to the Badia a Passignano, if you are parking for Walk 13. But the main tour turns *right,* heading very steeply down towards Greve. To visit the perfect little walled village of **Montefioralle** (🚻🏰🍷), park on the left, before the traffic lights, and walk through the arched gate in the wall.

When you reach the bottom of the hill, turn right at the main road to the centre of **Greve**★ (94km/58mi 🚻🏔🍴🍷🍷). Go left at the traffic lights, to the car park. Greve is a good place to catch your breath, have an ice-cream and shop for local produce in the arcaded Piazza Matteotti. From Greve retrace the SS222 via **Grassina** to **Florence** (111km). (Beyond Strada you will see signposting to Impruneta, if this is where you joined the tour.)

3 MARBLE MOUNTAINS OF THE ALPI APUANE, AND THE GARFAGNANA

A12 • Massa • Antona • Arni • Isola Santa • Castelnuovo di Garfagnana • Barga • Lucca • A11

96km/60mi; 3h30min driving from the A12 at Massa to Lucca

On route: Picnics (see **P** symbol and pages 8-11) 8, 9; Walks 6-8 (accessible via the *short-cut* route south of Arni), 9

This tour begins and ends on motorways, so is easily accessible. It is a tour of immense contrast — from the busy commercial coastal plain to barren mountaintops with no sign of habitation and then on to the historic city of Lucca. As the Alpi Apuane have been the source of much of the world's marble since Roman times, you will see the scars of magnificent marble quarries set in the most improbable locations. Yes, the rectangular 'bites' taken from the summits of mountains well over 1000 metres high are the quarries! The mountains themselves are magnificent, with extraordinary views in every direction, so wait for a clear day. While the mountain road is good, it is full of hairpins and precipitous drops, so it is not suitable for nervous driver or passengers, or for winter driving

Opening hours, information offices (*i*), and market days (⚖)
Carrara: *i* at The Civic Museum of Marble, Viale XX Settembre; tel: 0585 844403; ⚖ Mon (not on the main tour, best reached from the A12)
Massa: *i* at Via delle Pinete 270; tel: 0585 633115; ⚖ Tue
Castelnuovo: *i* at Piazza delle Erbe 1; tel: 0583 65169; ⚖ Thur
Seravezza: *i* at Via Corrado del Greco 11; tel: 0584 757325; ⚖ Mon
Barga: *i* at Piazza Angelio 4; tel: 0583 723499; ⚖ Sat
Lucca: *i* at Via Vecchia Porta San Donato; tel: 0583 442944; ⚖ Sat; Grotto del Vento, open daily from 1/4-30/9, Sun/holidays from 1/10-31/3; tel: 0583 722024; Castello Malaspina, open 09.30-12.00 and 16.00-19.00 Sat/Sun only; Orto Botanico (botanic gardens), Pietra Pellegrina, open daily 09.00-12.00 and 15.00-18.00; tel: 0585 4901

Take the A12 motorway towards Viareggio and Genova. This road runs north, parallel with, but not in sight of the Tuscan beach resorts. They are famous for miles of sand covered with rows of beach chairs and umbrellas. Leave the motorway at the exit for Massa*, and follow the signs for the town centre. As you negotiate this few miles of suburban sprawl, fill up before going into the 'petrol-free' mountains!

Massa (4km/2mi ◼🛖✕🏠M) is a marble town, where the great chunks of the stone are cut and worked before being transported elsewhere. As with the other towns in this area, marble is everywhere — buildings, sculptures, plaques … even pavements! The Malaspinas were the great family here; their impressive 11th-century castle is signposted along Via della Rocca. As you drive through Massa, look for the road to Terme di San Carlo and Pian della Fioba, taking care in the central piazza where you have to follow the signs carefully to get on to this mountain road.

*Or continue to the next exit, Carrara, if you wish to visit the Civic Museum of Marble. From Carrara centre take the road to Massa.

The climb begins immediately, on a good road which twists uphill in sweeps wide enough to accommodate the awesome lorries that bring down the marble. This is one of the most interesting roads in Tuscany, so take your time. As you climb, look back for the view over the coastal plain and the Castello Malaspina, but watch out for the cyclists, also awesome, as they begin their 1000 metre ascent.

Beyond **Terme di San Carlo** (7km; *P*8), where everyone seems to be carrying containers to fill with spring water, the magnificence of the high alps is evident. The lower slopes are clothed in heather, scrub and woodlands, interrupted occasionally by pretty, colourful villages clinging bravely to the slopes. Terraces, tiny stone houses, waterfalls, quarries with cascades of white stones tumbling down, are all crowned with irregular ridges of stone pinnacles, like rows of jagged teeth. Go through **Antona** (14km/8mi ♈), originally a medieval borough, where chestnuts are still important to the economy, and continue uphill until you arrive at the *rifugio* for the town of Massa and a wide parking area, at the entrance to a botanical garden of alpine and medicinal plants (❀ with guided tours only).

The road now penetrates a series of tunnels opening onto even more spectacular scenery. Be sure to stop in one of the few places where you can *safely* park, then have a good look round. To me it is extraordinary to find quarries almost at the summits of the mountains, testaments to great ingenuity and bravery. There are also a couple of picnic tables (⊼) on shady platforms along this stretch of road, and a tiny chapel dedicated to local men killed towards the end of World War II, when the Germans were making their last stand in Italy, along the 'Gothic Line'.

The highest point of the tour is the restaurant and *rifugio* 'Le Gobbie' (✕), at 1000m/3280ft. From here it is downhill all the way to Castelnuovo. Take time to stop at **Arni★** (28km/17mi ✕◾), the first village on the east side of the pass. In high summer, flowers cascade from the balconies of these grey houses, bringing a welcome splash of colour to the scene. If you would like to see some quarries at close quarters, take a road off to the left at the first bend (before the church with the tree growing from the tower). The tarmac ends in two minutes, at a parking area. From here the way-marked CAI 144 heads north along an old quarry track to the Sella Pass over the mountains. It's dusty, but you'll find this track fascinating; you'll keep wanting to reach the next bend, in the expectation of another derelict quarry, extraordinary rock formation, or view of the summit. Only two minutes from the parking area, take the second track on the left, to see an old quarry where the work looks as if it stopped only yesterday. There are great vertical walls of smooth marble, and precarious working platforms are pinned into the stone face, where a rope ladder still hangs down. Rusty huts, cutting gear, huge old tyres … even an old Cinquecento car, are scattered silent amongst the numbered blocks of marble waiting for transportation. Transportation that will now never come. It is a very evocative place.

Back on the tour, at the first T-junction after Arni you have a choice. If you wish to shorten the tour — perhaps to get to the start of Walks 6, 7 or 8 — turn right. After the Cipollaio Tunnel turn left, following hairpin bends down to the River Vezza. Follow the river downstream to Seravezza with its marble workshops, then go on to the A12 *autostrada* at Pietrasanta.

The main tour turns *left* towards the Garfagnana at this T-junction, passing a restaurant (✕) much used by truckers, set in the huge Henraux Quarry. From here on the quarries become fewer and the landscape changes. At first the mountain slopes are intimidating naked folds of solidified grey mud. The clothing of trees soon reappears. The road follows the river, which in places descends into a deep gorge. Steep-sided valleys join at both sides.

The river is dammed to make an attractive lake at **Isola Santa★** (32km/20mi ✕ ▄ *P*9; photograph page 72), where the longer version of Walk 8 begins and ends. To get to the shore and the lovely setting for Picnic 9, you have to leave your car in a lay-by before the village. Walk downhill for two minutes, to a gap in the wall on your right, from where a path leads to an almost-derelict village. Its tiny alleys, corners and archways make it attractive, but it is sad that it is being allowed to deteriorate in this way. The houses are roofed with local slate, not cut into neat squares, but left in irregular shapes as they came off the mountain. Though the church is falling down, the tower still has its bells.

From Isola Santa it is a steep descent via **Torrite** to **Castelnuovo** (45km/28mi ✝▮▄✕▄ ▄M) and the beginning of a gentle wide road running downstream alongside the lush River Serchio. This beautiful area is known as the Garfagnana. Follow signposting to the right, for Lucca and then Barga. (But if you would prefer to visit Tuscany's finest cave, full of stalactites, pits and abysses, rather than the pretty town of Barga, stay on the right-hand side of the river to Gallicano, then follow signposting to the right for the 'Grotto del Vento'. A narrow winding road takes you 9km uphill towards Fornovolasco. Stay on the road by the river.)

Those ready for a little civilisation should take the winding but no longer desolate road to **Barga★** (59km/37mi ✝▄✕▄▢▄⊓M). As you enter the village, there is park-

Views of the quarries and marble works around Carrara. See also page 65, 'Marble from the Alpi Apuane'.

ing on the piazza just over the bridge, above a park with picnic tables and a bar. To visit the simple but very beautiful cathedral, make your way up one of the many tiny streets. The cathedral, begun in 1000, is on a terrace above the town's rooftops and overlooks a splendid panorama of the Alpi Apuane. The rest of the town is delightful — very medieval, with its *palazzos* pushed close together, or separated by steps and 'snickets' running up and down the hill.

From Barga stay on the east side of the river, passing the junction with the road from Bagni di Lucca (69km/43mi; access to Walk 9) and joining the SS12 for Lucca. On the right now you will see the elegant, much-photographed Ponte di Maddalena, also called the 'Devil's Bridge'. Continue to the ancient city of **Lucca★** (96km/60mi ⚓🏨🏠✕📷🚉M) and the **A11 motorway**.

4 THE COOL HILLS AND FORESTS OF THE PRATOMAGNO, AND THE VALLEY OF THE CASENTINO

A1 motorway • Incisa • Reggello • Saltino • Vallombrosa • Montemignaio • Castel San Niccolò • Poppi • Bibbiena • Talla • Loro Ciuffenna • Castelfranco di Sopra • A1

119km/74mi; 3h30min driving

On route: Picnics (see **P** symbol and pages 8-11) 10, 11; Walks 10-12

To escape the summer heat, local people go to the sea or up into the hills. The Pratomagno is one of these places of refuge, though worthy of a visit at any time. It's accessible, quiet and almost as it has been for centuries, full of trees, rocks, water, wild life and forest tracks. This tour circles the Pratomagno hills via the Casentino, the upper valley of the Arno, where you find the charming town of Poppi with its castle.

Opening hours, information offices (*i*), and market days (♙)
Saltino-Reggello-Vallombrosa: *i* at Piazzale Roma 7; tel: 055 862003
Poppi: *i* at Via Nazionale 14, Badia Prataglia; tel: 0575 559054; ♙ Tue
Bibbiena: *i* at Via Berni 25; tel: 0575 593098; ♙ Thur

Leave the A1 motorway at the Incisa exit: turn right and right again, following the signs for Reggello. Leave this road to turn left, up towards the hills of the Pratomagno, with tall sand cliffs in the foreground. In the medieval town of **Reggello** (12km/7mi ✝︎✕�"), carefully follow signposting for Vallombrosa. The winding, wooded climb begins on the far side of the town. After the marble workshop in **Pietrapiena**, the road divides: go right. The road makes several long curves, one containing a large shady picnic table (🛱).

Go through **Saltino**, the summer retreat of the city workers from the Arno Valley, to **Vallombrosa★** (24km/15mi ✝︎▲▲✕ 📷�"), where the forest is filled with picnic areas linked by woodland tracks. The monastery of Vallombrosa is the centre of interest here; park just beyond it. While it has a church, shop and arboretum, what really attracts the visitors is the monastery's location amid cool woods and tumbling water. Walk 11 begins and ends here.

To continue the tour, return towards Saltino but, soon, turn left to take the road behind the abbey church, signposted for Secchieta and Montemignaio. Driving slowly, follow this very pretty road for 5km, past waterfalls and through beech woods. At a junction, turn right if you would like to make a 7km detour to the summit of Monte Secchieta, with its all-round views, bar, and parking for Short walk 12-1.

Otherwise, continue left downhill along a panoramic road to **Montemignaio** (33km/20mi ✝︎🍴▲▲✕📷🚙) and **Castello Alto Solatio**. Both these villages are now largely holiday centres, but Castello has great charm and antiquity, with its fort and cluster of tiny streets. Turn right in the village, with the castle tower high above you, and follow the SP70 signposted to Poppi and Arezzo. As you begin to descend, watch

24

for the signs at **Forcanasso** for the path to a Roman bridge. It's a 200m walk down to the bridge, a lovely spot with access to the stream for the agile.

Continue the tour along this scenic route that runs parallel with the river and crosses it a couple of times. When you arrive in the charming hamlet of **Castel San Niccolò** (43km/27mi ☗🚽✗🖳🖳🎏; cover photograph), park in the village centre if you would like to take a delightful 10-minute walk up to the castle. To get there, turn right along the main street, past the sculptor's studio, then go left to the river. Cross the old bridge and follow the stone track to the left, zigzagging up to the castle and a church tower with the biggest clock face you will probably ever see.

Still following signs to Arezzo, the route crosses the flood plain and the Arno. (At 48km, just after crossing the Arno, note the SS310 left to Stia: access to Walk 10; *P*10.) Entering Poppi from the north, turn right to cross the Arno again, and follow signs to the historic centre *('Centro Storico')*. The road goes up through the town, to the castle courtyard. There is parking there, but it is preferable to park below the castle walls and explore on foot. Old **Poppi★** (50km/31mi ☗🚽▲▲ ✗🖳🖳📷) has narrow arcaded streets lined with shops, some selling local copperware. The castle, reputedly the best-preserved medieval castle in the region, was modelled on the Palazzo Vecchio in Florence. If the children are with you, there is a 'Zoo Fauna Europa' south of the town.

Return to the bottom of the hill but, before crossing the river, take the SP65 — to either the right or the left, following signposting for Ortignano. This road circles Poppi to continue south, keeping to the right bank of the Arno. At the next intersection, turn left for Arezzo. Keep following signs for Arezzo, and you will skirt **Bibbiena** (59km/37mi ☗🚽▲▲✗ 🖳🖳), one of the oldest and most industrial towns in the area. It has a few interesting buildings in its old heart, including the Palazzo Dovizi and the church of San Lorenzo.

Still following Arezzo signs, there is a 6km-long stretch of busy road taking you through a commercial area. Then you leave the towns and begin to cross the southern end of the Pratomagno hills. Continue along the main road, SS71, but cross the river again at **Rassina**, and follow the pretty SP59 towards Talla. Turn sharp left in **Talla** (73km/ 45mi ☗✗🖳🖳), heading up through chestnut woods.

The route contours round the hills; ignore all roads down to the left. Some 9km from Talla, the road turns sharp left and down to San Guistino. *Don't* take this turning, but turn right after the stream, past a sign, 'Foresta Demaniale'. This is a *strada panoramica,* with views to the west between the trees. After the Fonte delle Lucciole (Fireflies' Spring), the road (✗)

Left: old bridge at Loro Ciuffenna. Right: the church tower at Castel San Niccolò has the biggest clock face you are ever likely to see. Below: old mill at Loro Ciuffenna, which you can visit by stretching your legs for 10 minutes.

divides: take the left fork for Anciolina, descending a narrow road through open heath between stone mountain hamlets. At one point the road bends sharply round, to face the steep slopes of the Pratomagno. Just beyond **Anciolina**, on a sharp curve, there is a stone-laid road on the left. It quickly leads to a stand of pines on a ridge, a perfect picnic place, with sun and shade and places to stroll.

After the third hamlet, **Treoane**, turn left at the intersection and drive to **Loro Ciuffenna**★ (102km/63mi ✝🏠✕🅿️🚃), a village on two sides of a very deep gorge, linked by a beautiful old bridge and less attractive new one. To stretch your legs for 10 minutes, park just before the bridges, walk across the new bridge, and turn right towards the information office. From there you can see a mill at the side of the gorge. Carry on under the bridge, along the side of the gorge, and cross back on the old bridge. This short walk is quite dramatic when the river is full. Before you leave the area, you might like to see the Romanesque church★ at Gropina (✝ 2km south, on the Arezzo road), with its huge campanile, three naves, columns decorated with tigers and birds and a very 'Dark Ages' pulpit.

The tour continues to Castelfranco, through an intensely-terraced landscape clad in olive trees (photograph page 84). This road (SP1), called 'The road of the seven bridges', links several medieval towns before arriving at Arezzo. **Castelfranco di Sopra** (112km/70mi ✝🏠✕🅿️🚃 **P**11; Walk 12) is one of these towns, walled and fortified as a military outpost by Arnolfo di Campio. The town is set in a landscape of eroded cliffs *(balze)*. If you would like to observe these great sandy cliffs (photograph page 86) more closely, take the short walk described at the right.

To return to the *autostrada* (119km), skirt to the right of Castelfranco, following signs for San Giovanni. Take the Valdarno exit to go south or the Incisa exit to go north.

Short walk at Castelfranco (40min-1h30min; easy; 🚗: park just at the edge of Castelfranco, on the road to Loro Ciuffenna, by a woodyard and opposite a furniture shop (see map pages 84-85). Take the track across the road, signposted to the Covo Restaurant. Watch for steps on the left, and take them down to a lower track. Follow the red and white CAI 51 waymarks to the right and down towards the stream (which you will hear but not see). Follow the track at the right of the Borro di Acqua Zollina (Sulphur Water Stream). You can turn back at the ford (20min), to shorten the walk. After about 40min, at a junction by a factory, turn right on another track, then go left over a bridge, to a sandy stream. Follow the stream bed, then turn left up the steep hillside, to a track. Keep right at a junction by houses. Skirt to the right of Castelfranco by taking Via Aretina towards the Loro Ciuffenna road and your car.

5 HILLTOP FORTRESS TOWNS WEST OF SIENA

Superstrada Florence-to-Siena • Monteriggioni • Colle di Val d'Elsa • San Gimignano • Volterra • Casole d'Elsa • Strove • Monteriggioni • Superstrada

111km/69mi; 3h30min driving

On route: Picnics (see **P** symbol and pages 8-11) 12, 13; Walks 18, 19

This tour explores the pleasant hills west of Siena via five hill-fortress towns and gentle roads seeking the high ground. In the height of the season some of the roads, especially around San Gimignano, will be busy. I recommend choosing only one town to explore, leaving plenty of time for a short walk in this glorious countryside.

Opening hours, information offices (*i*), and market days (🔄)
Monteriggioni: *i* at Largo Fontebranda 5; tel: 0577 304810
Colle di Val d'Elsa: *i* at Via Campana 43, part-time; tel: 0577 922791; 🔄 Fri
San Gimignano: *i* at Piazza del Duomo 1; tel: 0577 940008; 🔄 Thur
Volterra and the Val di Cecina: *i* at Piazza dei Priori 20; tel: 0588 87257; 🔄 Sat
Casole d'Elsa: *i* at Piazza della Liberta 1; tel: 0577 948705; 🔄 1st and 3rd Mon of every month

Monteriggioni has the capacity to transport you from the drama of the fast Florence-to-Siena *superstrada* directly into medieval times. The village itself is completely encircled by its high stone wall and protected by 14 towers. Although it was built in 1203, it shows little sign of ageing. In the mind's eye, the forces of Siena could well be behind those walls ready to repel the avaricious Florentines. Dramatic and evocative it certainly is, from the outside. Inside it is a typically sleepy Tuscan village. To get to **Monteriggioni★** (🏠✖️🖥️📷) follow the signs from the *superstrada* (also called the 'Raccordo SI-FI'). Parking is in the field below.

Return towards the *superstrada,* but take the left turn for Colle di Val d'Elsa, the second medieval fortified town. The modern town greets you first, with its glass factories. At the junction where both roads are signposted to Volterra, take the right fork, keeping the town on your left. Follow the Volterra signs; they lead to a winding road alongside the old city and the wall. As with all these fortified towns, space inside the walls is at a premium, and the alleys and tiny streets are *not* the place for visitors' cars. Outside the walls there is usually a well-signposted car park that allows entry to the town through one of the gates (usually after a bit of a climb). **Colle di Val d'Elsa★** (12km/7mi ✝️🏠✖️🖥️📷M) is well worth the climb, especially in the sleepy afternoons, when a hush prevails, and the lanes can make you believe you are back in the 13th century.

Continue on the road towards Volterra but, 3km along, turn right on a small road signposted to San Gimignano. As you cross the plateau of farmland, you will see the towers of this beautifully-preserved medieval city dominating the

TUSCAN FOOD

Tuscan food is the food of the peasants. It is very close to the countryside — basic farm produce, freshly cooked and simply prepared, to satisfy the appetites of farm workers. These basics are from foods which grow so well here — olives for oil, wheat for bread, meats, vegetables, and fruit. Wayside herbs are used to flavour the food and bring the smell of the country on to the plate.

Bread

Bread has always been the staple food of Tuscany, unlike in other areas of Italy where the staple foods are pasta, polenta or rice. Traditionally the family bread was baked once a week in a domed wood-burning oven. As the bread needed to keep for a week, no salt was added. This meant the bread didn't form mould; instead it became harder and harder. Italians have invented a multitude of recipes to make the old bread edible. Examples are *ribollita*, a vegetable and bread soup, and *pappa al pomodoro*, a sort of thick porridge of bread, fresh tomatoes, oil and garlic. Is it a lucky coincidence or just the good palate of the Tuscans that makes unsalted bread so good with other local produce: robust wine, tasty olives, salty prociutto and mature *pecorino* cheese?

Polenta

This yellow 'mush', made from corn (maize) flour, is used as an alternative to pasta, served with sauces, or left to set then sliced and fried. The arrival of corn from America, probably in the 16th century, had a major impact on the lives of the peasants. It could be planted after the wheat had been harvested, thus providing a double crop. Its large grains made flour for humans and good animal fodder. Soon it was a staple food in some areas, markedly lessening starvation. Sadly, when maize was imported into Italy it came without vital dietary information. In order to release an essential mineral, niacin, maize needs to be processed with ash, calcium bicarbonate, 'lime' or other mineral salts. Native Americans, who also used maize as a staple food, knew the secret: they baked it in the ash in their fires. But in Italy, without the release of niacin, a disease called pellagra developed, which became an epidemic in areas of great poverty — where polenta was almost the only food. Not only did the sufferers develop thickened skin, but it affected their brains. Asylums had to be built for the worst cases. It was not until 1905 that scientists verified the cause of the disease. Some historians believe that pellagra wasn't eradicated until the *mezzadria* (see page 57) ended, when peasants left the land and chose more varied diets.

---

landscape to the left. In medieval times, tall tower houses were status symbols demonstrating the wealth and power of the owners. They were common in many prosperous towns, especially as the towers were safer places to live when surrounded by warring neighbours. **San Gimignano★** (21km/13mi ✝️🏨🏔️✕🍴🚊♨️📷*P*12; Walk 18) at one time hosted over 70

Chevronned lane (right) and ploughed fields (above), both at Monteriggioni tower houses. The wealth of the town derived from pilgrims passing through en route to Rome from northern Europe. Today 15 towers remain, the tallest of which is the town hall and civic museum, open to the public. If you can, choose a quiet time to visit the town, not least because the many car parks can get full. Don't miss the back streets, and the Rocca Gardens, from where you will see the vineyard-clothed hills and woodlands descending to meet the city walls.

Continue on the main road, with the walls of San Gimignano on your right. At the northern end of the town, follow the sign to Gambassi, along a ridge road (*P*13). Turn left at **Castagno** and later (35km) turn left for Volterra. Join the main road just to cross the Era River, but then turn left on the secondary road Volterra. Half way up the hill, there are two right turns. The first, with little parking, leads to the ruined Camoldese Abbey shown on page 109 and views of vertical cliffs *(balze)*. The second turning, with a car park, also leads to the *balze* view (🎦) … and to the giant church of San Giusto that has dominated the horizon for centuries.

Volterra★ (53km/33mi ✝🍴🏔△✕�filling🅿🚉🎦M) is ahead, set on a Pliocene ridge protected by steep cliffs. It is one of the oldest cities in Italy and was once a large and powerful Etruscan town. Its wealth through the ages has been based on locally-found minerals: sulphur, salt, alabaster, alum, lead, tin and iron. Today Volterra is valued for many reasons, including the richness of its Etruscan remains (it has a fine Etruscan museum and many tombs to explore) and the alabaster that is mined and worked here. Most precious of all is the fact that within the walls Volterra is virtually unchanged since Pope Sixtus plotted to murder Lorenzo de Medici over the rights to mine alum.

The tour turns back from Volterra on the SS68 signposted to Florence. This road meanders beautifully through open country of cereals, vines and sheep. Some 12km along, turn right to **Casole d'Elsa** (76km/47mi ✝🍴🏔✕🚉🅿M), the fifth fortress town. Its role was to guard the upper Elsa Valley, and the town still has the air of a 'last outpost'. The car park is on the right. Walk left to the war memorial and find the steps above it, leading to the charming medieval centre.

Continuing east, take the right fork out of the town. At the main road, turn left, heading briefly towards Colle. But then turn right to **Mensanello**. At the main road go left; cross the river at **Santa Giulia** (102km/63mi), then turn right to **Strove**. This lane edges the deeply-wooded hills called the Montagnola. After passing **Castel Petraia** and the abandoned 12th-century abbey at **Abbadia Isola★** (✕🚉🅿), you have a magnificent view of Monteriggioni in the distance. Turn left at the main road to join the *superstrada* (111km).

6 THE DRAMATIC LANDSCAPE OF THE SIENESE CRETE

Siena • Asciano • Monte Oliveto Maggiore • San Giovanni d'Asso • Castelmuzio • Pienza • San Quirico d'Orcia • Buonconvento • Siena

142km/88mi; about 4h driving

On route: Picnics (see **P** symbol and pages 8-11) 14, 15; Walk 20

This tour is about landscape. Although the villages en route do have treasures of art and architecture, the real joy of this route is the scenery. The Sienese Crete (or Sienese 'Clays'; see photograph page 111) have been the subject of many paintings through the ages. Once sea bed, the mud of its floor is now clay, and the bones of its sea creatures have become limestone. Not much likes to grow on this poor clay soil so, unprotected by vegetation, it has been eroded into deep gullies and ravines. Dramatic though this is, even more beautiful is the gently curving plateau, especially in spring, when it is covered by a bright green blanket of new grass. In summer this turns yellow as the cereals ripen. By autumn the soils reappear, radiating their earthen colours while being ordered into line by powerful tractors. The whole is dramatically pierced by lone cypress trees, or series of cypresses, planted by a landscape architect of long ago. This tour could be combined with Tour 7 for a very long day, or you could end it with a thermal bath at Bagno Vignoni. Take your swimming things!

Opening hours, information offices (*i*), and market days (⚖)

Siena: *i* at Piazza del Campo 56; tel: 0577 280551; ⚖ Wed
Asciano: *i* at Corso Matteotti 18; tel: 0577 719510; ⚖ Sat
San Giovanni: *i* at Via XX Settembre 15; tel: 0577 823101; ⚖ 1st Mon of every month, in the afternoon
Pienza: *i* at Corso il Rossellino 59; tel: 0578 749071; ⚖ Fri.
Buonconvento: *i* at Via Soccini 32; tel: 0577 806012; ⚖ Sat
Bagno Vignoni: pool open every day, closed at lunch time.
Monte Oliveto: monastery open every day from 09.15-12.00; Gregorian Chant is sung at 18.00 in winter, 17.00 in summer

Leave Siena following the signs for the *autostrada* to Roma, the A1. Soon after the Siena bypass joins the cross-country road, turn right on the SS438, following signs for Asciano. You are now in the Crete, following a gently-winding route that keeps to the high land, allowing you broad vistas of continuous fields seductively curving over the earth's sur-

Monte Amiata, from the outskirts of Pienza

face like a thin sheet over a naked body. It is extraordinary; timeless, endless, beautiful. A strange gold and concrete monument on the left (9km/6mi) gives you an opportunity to park and stare for as long as you like (📷). Then continue through Siena's 'bread basket' to **Asciano★** (28km/17mi ✝ ▲ ✕ ☕ ▯ M), with its Etruscan beginnings and walls built by the Sienese in 1351.

Return the way you came into the town, but then turn left to the **Abbey of Monte Oliveto Maggiore** (35km/22mi ✝ ✕ ☕ 📷 🎍; Walk 20; photograph page 110). As with many monasteries, the monks have tried to make the natural environment part of the spiritual experience, so they encourage you to wander the woodland paths quietly. The giant brick monastery, with its famous frescoes by Luca Signorelli and Sodama, its church, library, court room and pharmacy, are all open to visitors.

From the car park return on the road by which you arrived, but turn right to **Chiusure** (39km/24m ✕ 📷 ▯P14). Some 300m/1000ft above the monastery, the village is typical of this area. Parking is outside the walls; it is better to explore the collection of medieval brick buildings on foot. The road circles to the left of the village, then continues through sheep country and woodlands to **San Giovanni**

Castelmuzio is totally untouristic, unchanged over the centuries — a bundle of alleys with a terrace outlook spanning a fine vista.

d'Asso (43km/27mi ♦️⛺️✖️🚉🍺; Short walks 20-1 and 20-2) with a fine 11th-century church. More noteworthy perhaps is the fact that this village has the highest percentage of truffle hunters in all Italy; 60 for every 900 of the population! They hunt white Sienese truffles.

From here follow signs for Trequanda. You cross the railway, which is now only used by tourists in the season. The road passes brick kilns making and selling garden ceramics typical of Tuscany. Leave the Trequanda road at **Montisi**, turning right towards Castelmuzio. The road descends steeply into and out of a wooded ravine, up to the tiny village of **Castelmuzio** (56km/35mi ⛺️📷🍺M), where it is well worth strolling inside the walls. Soon after leaving the village, don't miss the *very sharp* right-hand turn signposted to Pienza, just on a bend. This quiet road boasts a picnic site with tables and a pretty view (59km/37mi 🪑*P*15). To stretch your legs, there is a pleasant short walk just uphill from the picnic site, along a cypress-lined track to the monastery of Sant'Anna. The monastery was used as the setting for the film 'The English Patient'.

Continue until you meet the main road, the SS146, then turn left to **Pienza★** (83km/51.5mi ♦️⛺️✖️🚉🍺M), where there is ample parking around the walls. Although the town is really a working agricultural centre, it has an impressive heart. One of its famous sons, Pope Pius II, thought he would make it a monument of Renaissance architecture. He began grandiose plans to rebuild it all, but managed only to change its name to Pienza and to build a few very splendid palaces. What he did accomplish, however, is delightful, and is centred around the Piazza Pio II. Pienza is also famous for its sheep cheese, *pecorino,* and I hope you will try some.

Leave Pienza by following the walls, with the town on your right. The road drops down to travel south through more dramatic landscapes, where the extinct volcano, Monte Amiata, makes a distinctive backdrop. Follow the signs for Siena; go right at the crossroad to the SS2 (95km/60mi).

If you would like a little invigorating exercise before beginning your return, the thermal pool at Bagno Vignoni is just 2km along the road (take a left and then a right). Bagno Vignoni is described in Car tour 7 and Walk 22.

To return to Siena, turn right on the SS2 — an important arterial road, busy but still beautiful. Its other name is the 'Cassian Way', originally built around the year 220BC to join Rome with Fiesole. You pass through **San Quirico d'Orcia★** (♦️⛺️✖️🚉🍺) and **Buonconvento** (115km/71mi ✖️🚉🍺M), both historic walled towns now surrounded by modernity, before reaching **Siena** (142km/88mi).

7 AROUND MONTE AMIATA — VOLCANIC LANDSCAPE, HOT SPRINGS AND SKIING

SS2 • Montalcino • Sant'Antimo • Castelnuovo dell'Abate • Monte Amiata Scala • Seggiano • Pescina • Monte Amiata • Pescina • Vivo d'Orcia • Bagni San Filippo • Castiglione d'Orcia • Bagno Vignoni • SS2

105km/65mi; about 3h driving from the SS2

On route: Picnics (see **P** symbol and pages 8-11) 16, 17; Walks 21-24

Medieval walled towns, the most beautiful church I have ever seen, an extinct volcano covered with trees, and hot springs — not bad for a 65 mile circuit. The wine from this area is one of the best in Italy, and the panorama from Monte Amiata must be one of the best, if the day is good. There is a whole day's worth of exploration here.

Opening hours, information offices (*i*), and market days (⚖)
Montalcino: *i* at Costa del Municipio 8; tel: 0577 849331; ⚖ Fri
Sant'Antimo: abbey church open from 10.30-12.30 and 14.30-18.30
Abbadia San Salvatore (for Monte Amiata): *i* at Via Adua 25; tel: 0577 775811
Castiglione d'Orcia: *i* at Via Marconi 13; tel: 0577 887363; ⚖ on the 4th Sat of every month.

Leave the Siena-to-Rome road (SS2) at the signs for Montalcino, the walled hilltop town you see ahead. As the road climbs out of the wide valley, it passes through intensively-farmed land, rich especially in vines. This is the home of the famous Brunello di Montalcino wine. Keep the town on your right as you follow the walls round to the parking areas, then walk up into the old centre. **Montalcino★** (9km/6mi ✚🗡🏔 ✕🏠📷♨M), is a pleasant low-key place, with wine shops, walls and a 14th-century castle. Walk 21 begins here.

Leave the town from the junction below the castle, on the SP55 signposted to Sant'Antimo and Castel-nuovo. Drive slowly, as this road is surrounded by a landscape rich in pattern and variety. Just before reaching Castelnuovo dell'Abate on the hill, turn down right to **Sant'Antimo** (18km/11mi ✚), where there is parking. This sublime abbey, shown in the photograph on pages 116-117, sits in a bowl of fields and hills, and the church's simple interior provides the perfect surroundings for the Gregorian chant that is still sung by the monks. Walk 21 ends here. You might like to make a short, 35-minute circuit from here to Castelnuovo and back. If so, continue on foot along the track from the car park, towards a stream. Turn left before the stream to a grassy area (Picnic 16), then walk up the path to the road. Turn left, walk to a

View from Castiglione towards Monte Amiata, with an 'agriturismo' farm on the knoll

34

crossroads below the village and turn right to explore Castelnuovo or left back down the road to the abbey.

At the crossroads before Castelnuovo dell'Abate (19km/ 12mi ♣✕⌨️🍷) take the road to the railway town of **Monte Amiata** (28km/17mi 🍷), now with no trains. Cross the railway and the river, then head uphill towards Monte Amiata through sandy terrain eroded into organ-pipe shapes. Follow the signs for Monte Amiata Vetta (the summit) and Arcidosso via **Seggiano** (34km/21mi ♣🏨🏔✕🍷). Then take a left turn to the holiday village of **Pescina** (38km/24mi 🏔). From here it's a slow 12km drive up a winding road through beech woods to the summit of **Monte Amiata★** (50km/31mi 🏔✕ ⌨️🍷), Tuscany's only volcano (extinct, I hasten to add). The village is a typical ski resort with bars, restaurants, and lifts. A short walk leads from the car park to a viewpoint at the top: on clear days, this is really worth the effort — you can see half of Tuscany, as well as Elba, the Mediterranean and the Apennines from Umbria to Abbruzzo.

Return to **Pescina**, then turn right for Vivo d'Orcia. As you approach Vivo, turn right on an unsealed road signposted to a picnic area (⊓*P*17; pay parking in the season). Here in the beech woods are the springs that supply Siena with water, via an aqueduct built between 1908-1914. There is also the 13th-century Romanesque chapel shown on page 128, two 'drying sheds' used to preserve chestnuts, and waterfalls. **Vivo d'Orcia★** (71km/44mi ♣🏔✕🍷⊓*P*17; Walk 24), is one of the highest villages on the volcano. On its outskirts is the 'Contea di Vivo': this picturesque hamlet, with its church and villa, was once a monastery; later it earned its living

Bagno Vignoni; see also photograph page 118.

using water power for factories and furnaces, but the present hamlet bears no scars.

From Vivo head south on the road for Abbadia San Salvatore, but turn left at the main road towards Siena and on to **Bagni San Filippo★** (84km/52mi 🏨 ✕ 🍴). At this smallest of spas, the water is heated to between 25-52°C by the earth's hot inner layers which are close to the surface in this area. Follow the stream-side path to the spectacular Fosso Bianco, a series of calcium formations that looks like a chalk waterfall. If you would like to bathe, this spa also has a swimming pool and two natural pools, one hot, one cold. It is claimed that the water cures a multitude of ailments.

From here follow signs for Vivo d'Orcia via **Campiglia d'Orcia**, a village with a monument on a pinnacle. Past Campiglia, carry straight on at a crossroads, following signposting to Arcidosso. Then turn right along the ridge, to **Castiglione d'Orcia** (102km/63mi 🚻🏨🏨✕🍴📷🍴; Walk 23; photograph page 122). This truly medieval town has stone-paved streets and squares. A short walk to the castle dominating the town is rewarded by fine views that demonstrate its impregnable position. You can either walk or drive down to the hamlet of **Rocca d'Orcia**, perched on a cliff below Castiglione (photographs pages 105, 124).

Return to the Siena road. This part of the SS2 is where the medieval pilgrims' route, the Via Francigena, again joins the Roman Via Cassia to head north to Siena. (From Siena the Via Francigena then turns northwest for France and Canterbury in England.) Medieval road-builders had abandoned the Via Cassia's route from Rome in southern Tuscany in order to find safety and protection from bandits in this very wild area; they chose an upland route linking hilltop fortress towns such as Radicofani.

Just after crossing the River Orcia, follow signposting left to **Bagno Vignoni★** (105km/65mi 🏨✕🍴; Walk 22; photograph page 118), another tiny spa village. Parking is plentiful, so leave your car to explore the village, which has a pool instead of a piazza. The Medicis built the elegant portico, as they were devoted to bathing in these beneficial bubbling waters. Sadly, no one is allowed to bathe there today; you have to go to the nearby Hotel Posta Marcucci. If you have never swum in hot mineral waters out-of-doors, rest assured that it is one of life's great experiences!

8 SOUTHERN TUSCANY, FORGOTTEN SINCE THE ETRUSCANS

SS2 • Castell'Azzara • Sorano • Sovana • San Martino sul Fiora • Saturnia • Montemerano • Manciano • Pitigliano • San Quirico • Onano • Acquapendente • SS2

124km/77mi; about 4h driving

On route: Picnics (see *P* symbol and pages 8-11) 18, 19; Walks 25, 26

This is the part of Tuscany that excites me most. A relatively-unknown area, only now seeking to develop its tourist potential, its memorable landscapes and historical associations may surprise you. Many of the rich remains of past inhabitants — the Etruscans, the Romans and the people of medieval times — are just lying about awaiting your discovery. There are pathways cut deep in the rock as funeral routes for the Etruscans, cave dwellings inhabited since ancient times, and medieval castles built on 'impossible' summits. And then there are the tufa-top towns, where the houses seem to hang on to each other to make sure they don't all slip off the edge. The historical remnants are set in a variety of landscapes, from the slopes of a dead volcano to deep gorges plunging down from gentle plains. Some areas are intensively farmed and still luxuriant in summer with hedgerow flowers, while others are wild enough to be protected environments for birds of prey. The other advantages of southern Tuscany are the very quiet roads and wonderfully relaxed atmosphere.

Opening hours, information offices (*i*), and market days (⚖)
Castell'Azzara: *i* at Via Dante Alighieri 38; tel: 0564 951651; ⚖ Thur
Sorano: *i* at Piazza Busatti; tel: 0564 633099; ⚖ Tue
Sovana: *i* at Piazza Pretorio; tel: 0564 614074
Saturnia: *i* at Piazza V Veneto 8; tel 0564 601280
Manciano: *i* at Via Roma 2; tel: 0564 614074; ⚖ Sat
Pitigliano: *i* at Via Roma 6, weekends only; tel: 0564 614433; ⚖ Wed
San Quirico: *i* at Piazza Repubblica, next to the restaurant; tel: 0564 619335 or 0564 619025

Travelling from Siena, leave the main road (SS2) after 38km, following signposting to the right for Castell' Azzara. Turn left to begin the climb to the amazingly-large working town of Castell'Azzara (considering that it is at an altitude of 800m!). Much of this part of Tuscany was once sea-bed, with a deep bedrock base covered with soft clays, sand, and limestone. You will see the result as you drive up the winding road. The road seems not to be built on *terra firma* at all, but on *terra* that moves — especially after heavy rain. The poor road engineers obviously have a difficult job keeping a road surface at all, so drive *piano, piano* to the top. At **Castell'Azzara** (13km/8mi ✝🏛🏔✕🚰📷🍷) turn left immediately, rounding the town, to take the road towards Sorano. As you descend you will see spread before you southern Tuscany and part of Umbria and, if it is a clear day, Lake Bolsena.

Sorano★ (35km/22mi 🏛🏔✕🚰📷🍷M) is the first of the incredible towns built high on outcrops of dark volcanic tufa. A fortified rock, the Masso Leopoldino, towers over the

37

town, with the houses hanging in there more by faith than design — and all this suspended above three gorges and three rivers. Park at the entrance to the old town and walk up towards the Masso Leopoldino. The narrow road curves around the castle. As you return you will pass through a zone that has been subjected to landslides caused by erosion and the number of cellars dug in the tufa. In 1929 the inhabitants were evacuated and the town started to die. Miraculously engineers have since shown how the town can be made safe again, and work has begun: the crumbled walls and broken roofs are being renovated and the houses offered for sale.

Back in the car, descend towards Sovana. You can enjoy an excellent view of Sovana and the surrounding countryside (⌨🅰) from the signposted park at the top of the next cliff to the left. Then drive down into the deep gorge and up the other side. The car park for **Sovana★** (45km/27mi 🚼🎦🏨 ✕🍴🅿🍺M) is past the castle, round a sharp left turn. This most charming of villages is largely medieval, with Etruscan and Roman remains. Indeed it is the centre of one of the most outstanding Etruscan areas. The surrounding countryside is riddled with tombs, necropoli, wells, sacred pathways, and waterways hewn from the rock, many of which can be explored on foot from here (see Walk 25). Don't miss the impressive Romanesque cathedral down the tiny stone road to left of the town hall.

As you leave Sovana on the road to San Martino sul Fiora, you pass the signposted entrances to many Etruscan sites. A small entrance fee is sometimes charged. The road then descends to the Fiora River (49km/30mi) which is cool, clean and attractive — upstream. On the left-hand side of the bridge there is an ugly gravel works. Park on the right and follow the track down to the river bed. It is great for a picnic (*P*18; photograph page 10). There is no shade, but you can take a cooling dip in the one of the river pools.

As you drive along the San Martino road, the view to the north is over the plain with the distinctive form of an extinct volcano rising from it, Monte Amiata. Follow the road to **Saturnia★** (70km/43mi 🚼🎦🏨✕🍴🅿🍺; Walk 26). The village itself is up on the hill. The famous thermal waterfalls are further along the Manciano road. At the time of writing they were informal — just park and swim any time, free. But rumours suggest there are some plans to 'organise' them. Parking is just beyond the petrol station, on the bend.

Feeling reinvigorated, carry on through **Montemerano** to **Manciano** (82km/51mi 🎦🏨✕🍴🅿🍺M). The route now turns back left and east towards Pitigliano. Before dropping into the gorge across from Pitigliano, stop *(carefully; sharp bend)* at the church of the Madonna delle Grazie for the best view

Thermal waterfalls at Saturnia (detour on Walk 26)

of the town (📷; see photograph pages 12-13). **Pitigliano★** (100km/62mi ✝🛎🔺✖🚰💺M), is the second of the tufa-top towns. It is not perched, but sits securely on the top of a great tufa outcrop. The cliffs in this area are extraordinary, full of holes just like Swiss cheese. These holes were excavated initially by the Etruscans, but are now used for storage — great for keeping wine cool. Take time to explore the palace, the aqueduct, and the alleys of the centuries-old Jewish quarter. Walk 25 begins in Pitigliano.

There is one more fascinating place to visit before you end this tour. Leave Pitigliano via the SS74, following signs for Onano and Acquapendente, but then turn off left to **San Quirico★** (110km/68mi 🔺✖🚰💺). In the village piazza call at the information office, to pay your small fee to visit Vitozza (they will also give you a map). The road to the car park is just ahead on the left, marked with a yellow sign. It is then a pleasant woodland walk to explore the ancient settlement of Vitozza (🛎⌒🚏P19), where people lived in the caves from the Bronze Age until certainly 1783. The 180 caves along the 'main street' were home to a rural community that was quite self-sufficient. Along the woodland and streamside paths there are also the remains of a castle, a mill, a dovecote *(colombaio)*, and a cave church — even a picnic table or two and toilets.

Leave San Quirico the way you came, continuing north, then east on the SS74, but turn left at the junction for **Onano** (116km/72mi); then go on to **Acquapendente** and the **SS2** (124km).

● Walking

M aps and waymarks
The walking notes in this book, together with the **maps**, will give you all the information you need to complete the walks. But if you like to take an area map with you, the series I recommend is 'Carta di Sentieri e Rifugi 1:25,000'. These are available in good book shops, but they only cover certain areas. Italy was last surveyed many years ago, so don't be disconcerted if your map doesn't agree with my walking notes. It is most likely that the map is wrong.

CAI means 'Club Alpino Italiano'. Its members are the wonderful people who walk the lanes with pots of red and white paint. They mark the trail with the distinctive red and white flashes shown in the photographs on pages 2 and 133, as well as doing many other good things to help hikers. In general their waymarks are reliable, except occasionally when a local landowner has tried to obliterate them. Often you can still spot them, however. *If you are following a CAI trail and haven't seen a waymark for five minutes, you have probably missed the way.* A few other walks in this book follow locally-waymarked routes; if this is the case, I describe the waymarks. Bear in mind, however, that some of the walks only follow part of a waymarked route, so don't just follow waymarks without reference to the text!

R ight of way
You can walk almost anywhere in Tuscany. Because hunters have the right to hunt on any but fenced-off land, it seems walkers have the same privilege. Italians seem very relaxed about hikers. Although many of the paths, including CAI routes, are on private land, it is not usually a problem if you follow the Country code (see page 141). Signs indicating private property are there to deter motorised traffic.

Some paths that once led straight to the farm door are being rerouted, as the farms are renovated. If a path is fenced off, look for a new route which often follows the fence.

A word of caution
Tuscany's countryside is a wonderful playground. It is also where people live and work. As farming changes, so does the landscape. It is doing so now in many areas, espe-

---

Note that there is more important information for walkers in the Hints for walkers, starting on page 137.

cially in the Chianti. Derelict farms are being renovated, and scrub land is being ploughed up to become new vineyards. The walking notes were accurate at time of writing, but there is no guarantee that a path will not be ploughed up for a row of vines. Almost always there will be an alternative, especially if it is a CAI route. Seasons also bring about change; where the notes refer to a 'stream bed', you may come upon a real stream. Please allow for these seasonal adjustments when planning your walk. Then enjoy the challenge of finding your way, even if it isn't always exactly as planned.

Timings and distances
The timings are *guidelines* only, and may vary according to weather conditions, etc. The times do *not* include any breaks, other than catching your breath at a viewpoint, so **allow plenty of extra time** to stand and stare, and picnic.

The walking notes
As with recipes, it is better to read through *all* the walking notes before setting off, but if that is asking too much, at least read through one complete stage, so that the landmarks en route are firmly fixed in your mind. Relax until you get there, then read the next section completely. Treat the notes rather like clues in a treasure hunt.

Do refer to the map, as it will give you a feel for the general direction of the walk. Words can be ambiguous, and landmarks do occasionally change.

Unless the notes advise otherwise, always keep to the main trail, ignoring all other minor paths.

The words *path, trail, track* and *road* have specific meanings in the walking notes.

■ *Path* means footpath, not usually wider than 1m/3ft.

■ *Trail* is used for old routes, worn by time, for example, 'mule tracks'. These are generally 1.5-2m/4-6ft wide.

■ *Track* refers to an unsealed vehicle track, whether used by 4-wheel drives, farm vehicles or even motor cars.

■ *Roads* are surfaced. If there is clearly a maintained surface but they are not tarred, I describe them as *unsealed roads*.

Below is a key to the symbols on the walking maps:

═══ main road	●▸ spring, tank, etc	☥ church
──── secondary road	*P* picnic suggestion (see pages 8-11)	† cross, tabernacle
──── minor road		⊡ cemetery
──── unsealed road	00 CAI route number	戸 picnic site with tables
──── track, trail	☞ best views	
- - - - path, steps	🚌 bus stop	⚨ transmitting mast
6 → main walk	🚋 railway station	⊞ map continuation
12 → alternative walk	🚗 car parking	*i* tourist information
—400— altitude	■ building	☼ mill
	■ castle, fortress	∩ cave

1 FROM BIVIGLIANO TO FIESOLE

See also photographs pages 8-9, 10, 15, 50

Distance/time: 17km/10.6mi; 4h45min

Grade: moderate, with ascents of about 430m/1390ft overall, otherwise mostly downhill. Suitable all year round, except in high summer

Equipment: as pages 137-138; also walking boots if the ground is wet

How to get there: SITA 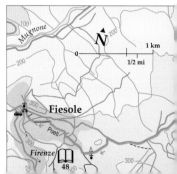 from Florence to Bivigliano; journey time 45min

To return: ATAF 7 from Fiesole to Florence; journey time 30min

Refreshments: bars at Bivigliano, Monte Senario; bar/restaurant at L'Olmo

Short walks

1 Bivigliano — Monte Senario circuit (6km/3.7mi; 1h45min). Easy; equipment as pages 137-138; access as main walk or by car: park in the wide square before Bivigliano (the 24km-point in Car tour 1). Follow the main walk to the T-junction (1h25min-point), then turn right for Bivigliano. At the main road in the village turn left for your bus or car.

2 Bivigliano — Monte Senario — Vetta le Croci (7km/4mi; 2h15min). Easy, with ascents of 225m/735ft, otherwise downhill. Equipment and access as main walk; return on SITA 308 back to Florence. Follow the main walk to Vetta le Croci, then turn right to the bus stop.

This walk leads you from Heaven to Earth, as it starts with a climb to the holy sanctuary of Monte Senario perched on a hilltop and then descends via a series of ridges to the historic but worldly village of Fiesole. It is one of my favourite walks because it keeps to the high ground. The land spreads before you like a giant carpet, starting at your feet and ending only where the horizon meets the sky. The path itself has recently been christened 'Via degli Dei' — Way of the Gods. If you have only time to do one walk in Tuscany, then choose this one, because it gives you a taste of everything these hills offer: vast panoramas of endless horizons, steep wooded hillsides, holy places, old farms, gentle olive groves, and imposing villas. There are places to linger and look about you, and other sections where you can really get into your stride and pound down the lanes. When you return to Florence, you can point to the distinctive shape of Monte Senario on the far horizon and say, 'I walked from there'.

Start the walk from the BUS TERMINUS at the spacious piazza in **Bivigliano**. Follow the main road into the village. There is a bar on the left, a good place for a morning coffee if you had an early start. Continue on the main road, watching out for a road on the right called POGGIO CHIARESE (on a sharp bend; **10min**). Take this road (CAI 18 WAYMARKS); it soon becomes a track and climbs left into the woods, to a junction of paths where the CAI 18 divides (**15min**). Follow the right-hand path uphill. Watch for the red and white way-marks as there are many other paths here. As long as you are climbing, you will reach the RIDGE TRAIL (CAI 00; **45min**).

Turn right along the ridge but, 15 minutes along, turn left off the main trail, following the red and white waymarks (**55min**). When you come to a little meadow (the setting for Picnic 3), the route veers to the right and meets the road up to the monastery. Follow the road uphill. Just before the bar and monastery, note Via della Preghiera del Silenzio on the right: this will be your ongoing route.

After visiting **Monte Senario** (**1h15min**; history overleaf) return to VIA DELLA PREGHIERA DEL SILENZIO and follow it downhill. It is the route to the cemetery and steps straight downhill below the monastery wall, past the Stations of the Cross and through an austere pine plantation. Imposing gates mark the end of the church land.

At this point you will meet a bend of the road

The Sanctuary of Monte Senario was founded by seven holy men from Florence in 1241, on a high hill (815m/2673ft) given to them by the nobleman Giuliano di Bivigliano.

They first built cells so they could become hermits separated from the world. Later other pious men were inspired to join them, and the Order of the Servants of the Holy Lady was formed. The church was consecrated in 1717, and the original hermits were canonised in 1888.

Today the buildings are a working monastery, used especially for spiritual retreats. The area has many grottoes, tabernacles and hermits' cells that can be discovered by exploring the paths around the monastery.

Carlina on the slopes of Monte Pratone, in the evening sun

leading back to the monastery. Just before continuing downhill, turn left to visit the huge ice house shown opposite. If you go round the to the back of the building, you can see inside it, to where the ice was stored.

Then return and follow the road down to a T-JUNCTION (**1h25min**). Turn left left towards 'FIRENZE'. *(But for Short walk 1, turn right.)* Continue along the road for about 2km (watching out for traffic), until you see a monument with an IRON CROSS (**1h45min**) on the left, set in a little clump of cypress trees. Take the path to the left here (it is still the red and white WAYMARKED CAI 00), up towards the clump of trees capping the hillock. The path circles to the left of the hill just before the summit (photograph pages 8-9), then heads down towards a reservoir in the distance. As you approach the main road, watch out for a right turn in the fields and take it, meeting the main road just above the crossroads of **Vetta le Croci** (**2h15min**). *(Short walk 2 ends here, turning right along the main road to a bus stop at the crossroads.)*

Cross the road at the 'FIESOLE' sign and take the path through the field opposite (photograph page 15, top right), walking uphill and parallel with the long side of the reservoir — a much-favoured picnic spot with city dwellers. You are now heading towards the ridge on your right, which will lead you to Monte Pratone. When you meet a second road, cross it and go left on VIA MASSETO. Now you are following the CAI 2, which turns right and rounds a house. Continue on to a third road, cross it, then follow it uphill a short distance.

Beyond the road sign, the way-marked CAI 2 (also signposted 'VIA DEGLI DEI' (**2h45min**) continues to the right, on a ridge path to the summit.

The summit of **Monte Pratone** (702m/2302ft; **3h45min**; Picnic 2) hosts a monument extolling the virtues of this beautiful spot, as well as a fire look-out tower. Head down past the RADIO RECEIVING STATION, join a gravel track, and walk on down to a road (**3h50min**). Turn right downhill, with views towards Fiesole.

When you come to a T-JUNCTION (**4h15min**), turn left on the rather busy road to Fiesole. To avoid the traffic through the village, I suggest you take the back road which is a little longer but much more pleasant. Five or so minutes down the main road, turn left uphill at a junction, following the sign to the camp site. When you are almost at the top of the hill, ignore the right turn into the camping ground and continue down to a T-junction. Turn left here and, a short way along, turn right uphill at another junction. At the next, more complicated junction, take the second street on the right (VIA F POETI). At the end of the handrail, where the road opens out, you will see a terrace, from which a tarred trail runs off to the left. Take this. Continue downhill and turn right at the T-junction, to the PIAZZA AND BUS STOP in **Fiesole** (**4h45min**). (Don't worry if you miss any of these charming back lanes; if in doubt, any right turn will bring you onto the main road to the centre.)

ICE HOUSE
This extraordinary structure was built in the 1880s by the monks of Monte Senario. It is thought to be one of the largest surviving ice houses in Europe. While most of the others were used to store ice for cooling drinks in summer, this one served an altogether different purpose. Placing ice on painful areas of the body was one of the few methods of pain relief known at that time.
The building itself was originally very elegant, faced with marble and stone and topped with a cupola above the dome. Filling it with ice during the winter was not difficult, just laborious. The monks built small ponds near the ice house. During winter nights, the temperature dropped, turning the pond water into ice which they collected and stored. The monks then loaded the ice onto carts and made regular trips to the hospitals of the city — truly 'angels of mercy'.
There are now plans to thoroughly restore this unique building.

2 CIRCUIT FROM FIESOLE VIA SETTIGNANO AND VINCIGLIATA

See also photograph page 101   Distance/time: 17km/10.6mi; 4h20min

Grade: easy, except for one steep rocky path that can be disconcerting for inexperienced walkers. Ascent of 120m/400ft. In spite of the long description, the walk is always within sight of Florence, so it is difficult to get lost. Suitable all year round.

Equipment: as pages 137-138

How to get there and return: ATAF 🚌 7 from Florence to/from Fiesole; journey time 30min. Or 🚗: park in the pay parking area in the square in Fiesole (the 8km-point on Car tour 1)

Refreshments: 'La Capponcina' near the main square in Settignano is a restaurant/pizzeria with charm and good food (especially the desserts). Across the road the old *drogheria* (grocers), is now a somewhat pricey *enoteca* (wine bar with food) — perfect for a good glass of wine and a plate of home-made pasta; it is called 'La Sosta del Rossellino' and is on the street of the same name.

Short walk: Fiesole — Settignano (6km/3.8mi; 2h15min). Easy; equipment and access as main walk. Return on ATAF 🚌 10 from the piazza in Settignano to Florence; journey time 25min. (If you have left your car at Fiesole, leave 🚌 10 at Ponte al Pino, walk back to the traffic lights and cross the road to Via Pacinotti, where there is a stop for 🚌 7.)

This walk is amazing in that it is always within sight of the city of Florence yet traverses real countryside with a variety of terrain, from steep rocky woodland paths to gentle meanderings through olive groves. The path links two communities bursting with history, works of art, and restaurants. From Fiesole you climb to Monte Céceri through the old quarry area of Florence, from where the stone *(pietra serena)* for many of the great buildings of the city was hewn.

Dramatic rock faces, old mule tracks and the remains of buildings make the path through the ilex and cypress woods all the more interesting. A monument to Leonardo da Vinci on the summit of Céceri tells of his experimentation with flight from this very spot. Perhaps he also came just to marvel at the magical landscape of cypress woods and fairy-tale castles. The quarry area extends to Maiano, where the stone-cutters lived and where Michelangelo was supposed to have developed his love of stone while being wet-nursed in nearby Settignano. The second part of the walk leads through traditional olive-growing farmland, passing the farm where some scenes from 'Room with a View' were filmed (but not among fields of violets, as in the book, but fields of corn).

One of the 'fairy-tale castles' is almost on the walking route and worth a short detour. It is the Castello di Vincigliata, complete with crenellated tower and battlements ... and a 'visitors' book' engraved on stone plaques on the wall. Talk about name dropping! To make a wonderfully full day, wander along Via del Rossellino in Settignano to famous Villa Gamberaia. The beautifully-maintained garden is

46

Fiesole sunset ; right: fountain and well at Stazzema, near Walk 7

usually open to the public on weekdays. You have to ring the bell at the gate and pay an admission charge.

Start the walk in the main square at **Fiesole**: with the cathedral on your left, walk uphill to Via G Verdi. Take this, following red and white CAI waymarks up past the panoramic view of Florence. Turn left onto Via di M Ceceri by the tiny corner house where the architect Frank Lloyd Wright once lived. From the top of this short climb you will see Monte Céceri in front of you. Walk downhill, then turn right onto a gravel track, Via degli Scalpellini (Stonemasons' St; **10min**), which leads into the woods. Continue past a little tabernacle, following the CAI marks and ignoring the many other old trails on each side. You are now climbing to the summit, so be sure to turn left off the main trail, following the CAI waymarks up the steep narrow path to the top of **Monte Céceri** (414m/1358ft; **20min**), where you will find the monument to Leonardo da Vinci. Catch your breath and admire the view, but keep back from the steep drop at the edge.

Cross the earthen piazza and find the start of the waymarked CAI 7 dropping steeply down towards Maiano. This is a fairly narrow and

STONEMASONS

Stone is the building material of Florence and district, from cattle troughs to cathedrals, from field walls to finely-sculptured fireplaces. These have been cut from the *pietra serena* ('serene stone') from quarries like the one at Monte Céceri. The stone was particularly valued for its gentle grey-blue colour, its resistance to the weather and its ease of working.

The stonemason or *scalpellino* was, for many generations, part of a closed society of manual workers. He would have been given his first chisel at the age of six by his father from whom he learned the trade. Stonemasons and their families lived together close to the quarry, at Settignano or Maiano for instance, marrying only within their community. Irving Stone's book, 'The Agony and the Ecstasy' gives a vivid description of the lives of stone masons in the time of Michelangelo.

47

[Handwritten note:] DO NOT TAKE THE ROAD NEXT TO THE CATHEDRAL. TAKE THE ONE FARTHER TO THE RIGHT. VIA VERDI IS RIGHT AT THE TOP OF THE PIAZZA.

rough, but well-marked path on the wooded hillside. The path zigzags, but veers generally to the left. At a THREE-WAY JUNCTION (**50min**) with directional arrows painted on a wall, follow the signs to Maiano: turn sharp right along a gently-sloping trail. Ignore the next three left turns; take the fourth turning left, following the CAI 7. The rocky trail ends at a junction with the unsealed ROAD FROM MAIANO (**1h10min**).

The next part of the walk, to Vincigliata, is not CAI way-marked. Turn left on this unsealed road for one minute. At a Y-junction, fork right and continue to a second Y-junction. Go right again, cross the stream, and rise up to the old FARM where 'Room with a View' was filmed (**1h15min**). The track takes you behind the barn. Almost immediately after the house, fork right on a narrow, flat path. You are now walking around the bowl of the valley towards the Castle of Vincigliata. Cross a stream on a wooden plank and continue to the right, through the woods. Stay on the rocky path, keeping left at all junctions, and gently climbing all the time. Go straight across a wider trail onto a narrow path along a terrace. This path ends at a T-junction with a track. Turn right downhill between the olive groves, then walk up to a ROAD (**1h45min**). Turn right downhill and pass the church in the hamlet of **Vincigliata** (photograph opposite, top). Your ongoing route is the next left turn (with a bar gate) but, if you have time, continue to the CASTLE described opposite.

The CAI 1 WAYMARKS reappear in Vincigliata: follow these through and round the olive groves and down onto a dirt track. Turn left and wend your way between a renovated farm and its chapel, to a smart villa (POGGIO AL VENTO). Beyond this house, at a JUNCTION (**2h**), take the first turning on the left, a very eroded trail among cypress trees. Go straight ahead

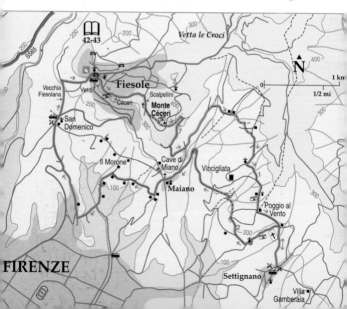

over a crossroads, following VIA DESI-
DERO DI SETTIGNANO (**2h05min**) to the left
of the park and the cemetery shown on
page 101. Coming to a T-junction in
Settignano, turn right to the PIAZZA
(**2h15min**). *(The Short walk ends here.)*

To continue the main walk, return to
the park by the cemetery and turn left
along the road at the top of the park, with
Settignano on your left. This attractive
road has good views over Florence.
After five minutes you reach a bend in
the road to accommodate a tiny chapel
and a villa. Almost immediately past the
bend, take the first dirt track on the right
(CAI 2), up into an olive grove. Beyond
the start of a WIRE FENCE (**2h35min**), the
trail turns diagonally right uphill into the
woods, below a shaly cliff. Leave the
CAI path when it turns steeply uphill to
the right: continue round the right-hand
bend to where the path divides, then
keep straight ahead, dropping gently
into the trees. Stay with this soft woodland trail, veering to the left, with a steep
drop on the left (you should not head
right until you have crossed the stream).
Cross a STREAM (**2h48min**) and turn right
just beyond it. Then go left immediately,
taking a rocky path uphill, towards a
stand of cypress trees. The path isn't too
clear at this point, but head uphill along
a faint path where the cypress trees meet
some umbrella pines. If you have a
compass, the direction is NW. After two
minutes your path meets a trail which
you follow left to the VINCIGLIATA ROAD
(**2h55min**).

Cross the road to a bar-gate and
descend the track beyond it through
fields, past an OLD MILL and over a bridge.
Beyond the stream, curve round and up
to a ROAD (**3h10min**). Follow the road a
short way left to **Maiano**, with its church,
villa and *fattoria*. The *fattoria* (see article
page 105) sells local produce, but also
houses a workshop for the restoration of
tapestries and the like.

**CASTELLO DI
VINCIGLIATA**
The original castle
on this site, owned
by the Alessandri
family, was des-
troyed in 1361. The
Alessandris had
fortified it well, as
they were constantly
feuding with the
family at the nearby
Castello di Poggio.
After it was aban-
doned, its ruins lay
untouched until
1840, when a
wealthy English-
man, Lord John
Temple Leader,
discovered it and
decided to restore it
to its medieval
splendour. He also
planted acres of
cypress trees, to
ensure a truly
romantic setting.
Today the castle,
almost as it was in
Leader's time, can
be hired for private
parties, but is only
open to the public
occasionally.

From the *fattoria* continue down the hill to the first house on the right (**3h20min**). Just *before* the house, turn right on a gravel track that starts in an olive grove. This takes you down past a second house (on the left), and you cross a stream on a tiny bridge. At the gate for the VILLA IL MORONE turn left and follow the road to where it divides (**3h40min**). A left turn would take you down to a bus stop (bus 17 for Florence). Turn right here to begin the climb back to Fiesole (keep uphill at all junctions). At **San Domenico** (**4h**) there are bars, a good pizzeria and bus stops for Fiesole and Florence. To complete the circuit on foot, cross the road, walk uphill, then go left on VIA VECCHIA FIESOLANA, the 'old road': it leads past interesting historic stonework back to the centre of **Fiesole** (**4h20min**).

Piazza Mino at Fiesole

3 CIRCUIT FROM CERCINA VIA MONTE MORELLO

See also photograph page 97   **Distance/time**: 19km/12mi; 5h30min

Grade: moderate, with an overall ascent of 600m/2000ft. The route is along quiet country roads or well-worn trails in woodlands and shady for two-thirds of the way. You must be sure-footed: one tricky descent demands agility. Suitable most of the year, except in high summer or the middle of winter.

Equipment: as pages 137-138

How to get there and return: ATAF 🚌 14 from Florence to/from Piazza Dalmazia; journey time 20min, then ATAF 🚌 43 to/from Cercina; journey time 20min. (This bus continues to Pian di San Bartolo on the Via Bolognese, where there are also buses to the centre of Florence.) Or 🚗: park by the church in Cercina, 5km west of Pian di San Bartolo: the road is signposted from the Via Bolognese (SS65) some 9km north of Florence, nearing the end of Car tour 1.

Refreshments: Bar/restaurants at Ceppeto and at Piazza Leonardo da Vinci. The bar at Ceppeto does good *schiacciata* sandwiches and has a fire in winter.

Short walks (both omit the ascent of Monte Morello)

1 Ceppeto — Poggio del Giro — Ceppeto (5km/3mi; 1h15min). Quite easy, with an ascent of 200m/650ft; equipment as pages 137-138. Access by 🚗: park at the bar at Ceppeto, 3.5km up the Monte Morello road (leave the Via Bolognese at a junction signposted to Monte Morello, 2.5km north of the cemetery at Pian di San Bartolo). Follow the main walk from the 40min-point to the major junction at the 1h10min-point. Then take the wide track to the right (CAI 6) back down to Ceppeto.

2 Cercina — Poggio del Giro — Cercina (9km/5.6i; 2h30min). Moderate, with an ascent of 400m/1300ft, but you must be sure-footed for the tricky descent from the Piazza Leonardo da Vinci; equipment as pages 137-138; access as main walk. Follow the main walk as far as the 1h-point. Here continue straight down the CAI 0 to the road and Piazza Leonardo da Vinci on the right. Pick up the main walk again at the 4h-point.

What is extraordinary about the valley of the Terzolle River is that it has existed almost unchanged for more than 500 years, and yet it is so close to Florence. On a clear day — the sort of day when colours seem to vibrate in front of your eyes — you feel you could just lean forward from Cercina and touch the Duomo in Florence. It looks so close. The walk takes you round one side of a fertile bowl of land at the head of the Terzolle Valley and then climbs through wooded slopes to the summit of Florence's highest mountain, Monte Morello. Initially you walk through a timeless landscape where farming has continued unchanged down the centuries. You pass a feudal castle, a stone church with its own miracle-maker, and unrestored farmhouses where olive oil is still made according to the old traditions.

During the climb through rough woodlands, look out for the remains of terraces once used for farming. People actually tried to feed themselves from this very unpromising

THE PARISH CHURCH AT CERCINA

The church of St Andrea is one of the oldest in the diocese of Florence. Its buildings have not been substantially changed since the 11th century, except for the addition of the portico in Renaissance times. Though it is a country church, built simply of local stone, it is quite rich in frescoes and carvings. The stonework around the main door is particularly fine. Sadly the frescoes in the portico have been almost ruined by rain. The one on the right tells the story of St Andrea, while the other describes the story for which this church is famous: the miraculous arrival of the statue of the Madonna and Child which stands in the church, in a niche to the left of the altar. It seems that a certain French cardinal wanted to take this carving to Rome. He set off on the tortuous journey over the Apennines, but rested a while near Cercina. There the mule carrying the statue positively refused to continue. Eventually the bishop decided to trust to the mule's judgement. It eventually moved towards the door of this church, where it and its precious load were honourably received. Everyone agreed that this was indeed a miracle. A place of honour was provided for the statue which has since been responsible for many more miracles.

land. On the summit ridge, with its panoramic views, you can get a real sense of the geography of Florence. Then it is a downhill stroll all the way back. Well almost!

Start the walk at **Cercina**, in front of the CHURCH. If the church is open, do not resist the urge to seek a few minutes of quiet inside. Cross the road and take the rosemary-lined VIA DELLA FONTACCIA, which starts opposite the church parking area. At the T-junction beyond a farm, turn right. Follow this road as it gently climbs up the foothills of Monte Morello, past a modern house decorated with a fresco of the grape harvest. Where Via Fontaccia becomes VIA PALAI (**15min**), you will see on the right a straight cypress-lined drive to the important old villa of Castiglione. (If you are as inquisitive as I am, you will wander a short way along here for a closer view at this historic villa.)

Then continue along the road until you reach a busier road and follow it to the left for five minutes, to **Ceppeto** (**40min**). This area, which is now largely a car park and picnic spot, was an important junction of many ancient roads. It is marked by the tiny stone chapel of **San Jacopo**, dating from the 11th century. Walk past the bar and past the roads on either side of it, but watch out for your path which starts further round the bend, on the right. Take this path (the red and white WAYMARKED CAI 00) up through the woods. It is a steep climb. Where the path flattens out for a while, there is a good view of Monte Morello and the nearby lower hills. The summit of your initial climb is **Poggio del Giro** (**1h**), with a little community of radio masts but no view.

Turn right here, still on the CAI 00. *(But for Short walk 2, go straight ahead down the CAI 0 to Piazza L da Vinci.)* Descend the well-waymarked CAI 00 to a MAJOR JUNCTION (**1h10min**) where you go straight ahead on the main trail to begin the ascent of **Monte Morello**. *(But for Short walk 1, turn right at this junction, following the CAI 6 track back*

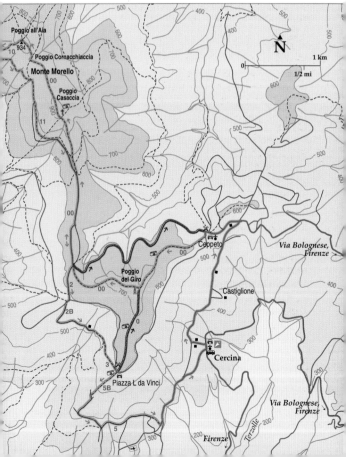

down to Ceppeto.) A track and then a path take you up to **Poggio Casaccia** (**1h55min**). Keep on up via **Poggio Cornacchiaccia** to the highest peak, **Poggio all'Aia** (934m/3063ft; **2h30min**), marked by a wooden cross.

To continue the walk, descend the CAI 10 on the western side of the summit. Five minutes downhill, turn left on the CAI 11 (*not* waymarked). This path contours along the hill and rejoins the CAI 00 (**3h10min**). At the MAJOR JUNCTION (first encountered at the 1h10min-point; **3h33min**), veer right on a wide track, the CAI 2. Cross a road and pick up another track (CAI 2B), offset a short way to the right. In front of a FARM (**3h50min**), the route (now a path, the CAI 3) starts to climb through trees. When you reach the **Piazza Leonardo da Vinci** (**4h**), take time to absorb the fine view over the whole of Florence.

Your next path (CAI 5B) begins opposite the bar at the piazza, almost dropping off the edge of the road. Initially it is quite tricky walking, as it is so badly eroded. Go straight downhill, following the waymarks and ignoring other paths. At the T-JUNCTION with a stony trail (**4h40min**) turn left, still on the CAI 5B. This drops steeply to a second T-junction by a PYLON: again go left on the CAI 5B. Reaching a 5-way junction at a wide bend in the track, leave the CAI 5B and carry on along the MAIN CONTOURING TRACK (CAI 5; **5h**). When this wide track turns right, keep straight ahead along a cart track (CAI 5). Ignore the 'no entry' sign (for vehicles only). Passing the gates to summer houses, you come to a sharp bend. Turn left here on a PATH (CAI 5; **5h05min**). (If you approach a round red and white 'no entry' sign, you have missed the path. It is only one minute back.) Meeting a ROAD (**5h10min**), turn left and follow it back to the CHURCH at **Cercina** (**5h30min**).

View from Cercina towards the hills above Fiesole

4 CIRCUITS AROUND SAN PIERO A SIEVE AND TREBBIO

See also photograph page 15   **Distance/time**: 22km/13.8mi; 6h

Grade: moderate, on account of the length; otherwise easy, mostly gentle climbing (about 400m/1300ft overall) on tracks and trails. As much of the route is shaded, it is suitable on fairly hot days and in any season.

Equipment: as pages 137-138; also optional bathing things (the pool at the Mugello Verde campsite is open to the public)

How to get there and return: SITA 🚌 302, 303, or 🚂 from Campo di Marte station in Florence to/from San Piero a Sieve; journey time about 45min. Or 🚗: Park on the main road in San Piero, by the river (the 37km-point in Car tour 1).

Refreshments: none on route

Short walks

1 San Piero — Tagliaferro (7.5km/4.7mi; 2h20min). Moderate, with an ascent of 200m/650ft. Equipment as pages 137-138; access as main walk. Follow the main walk to Tagliaferro and return to Florence or San Piero by SITA 🚌 302 or 303 (or 🚂 from nearby Campomigliaio).

2 Circuit from Trebbio (7.5km/4.7mi; 2h). Easy; equipment as pages 137-138. Access by 🚗: following Car tour 1 north from Florence, at the 35km-point follow signs for the autostrada (don't go into San Piero). Then watch for signs on the left to Trebbio and follow the motorable track to the castle. Park at the castle and follow the main walk from the 3h-point to the 5h-point, where you will arrive back at the castle.

3 San Piero — Tagliaferro — Trebbio — San Piero (14.5km/9mi; 4h). Moderate, with an ascent of 400m/1300ft; equipment and access as main walk. Follow the main walk, but omit the circuit west of Trebbio.

This hike is around the hills on either side of the River Carza. This valley is an important link between Florence and the Mugello, thus it contains a busy road and a railway line. But you will rarely be within sight or sound of either. Your views will encompass distant hills, pastures rich in lush grass, stone farmhouses, gentle woodlands and the evocative castle at Trebbio. On the homeward journey there is the possibility of a swim at the Mugello Verde campsite and an exploration of the huge Medici fort shown on page 15.

Start the walk on the main street at **San Piero**: find the CHURCH that backs on to the river. Take the narrow road on the north side of the church (the side furthest from Florence); it is the road to the cemetery. You cross the **River Carza** on a footbridge and then walk alongside the river, before going through an underpass beneath the railway station and arriving at the CEMETERY. Turn right at the junction by the cemetery and follow a road that first bridges the main road and then turns right back towards it. Take a left turn just before you reach the main road (**10min**). As you follow this narrow road past a HOUSE WITH THE NUMBER '12A' ON THE GARAGE, look for TWO YELLOW DOTS waymarking the Bologna to Firenze (BO-FI) walk. Follow these waymarks on this part of the route, climbing up to the ridge and then walking along it, parallel with the valley to your right.

At the next HOUSE, NUMBER 32 (**25min**) you reach a junction: take the lower, left-hand track here (signedposted as private property and with a wooden barrier, but waymarked with the YELLOW DOTS). Relax, enjoying the shade and the tranquility, but *at any important junctions, follow these waymarks, keeping to the top of the ridge!*

Watch out for your sharp right turn deep into the trees (**1h**); it takes you past a boundary stone marking the meeting of two boroughs, Borgo San Lorenzo and San Piero (**1h 05min**). Ignore the trail veering off to the right; follow the yellow dots and the sign 'VIA DEGLI DEI'. This narrow path keeps to the ridge. At a junction (**1h30min**) take a narrow and overgrown path descending to the right; it bears CAI RED AND WHITE MARKINGS. *Be sure to check after every junction that you are still following the red and white waymarks!* Ten minutes along the path, when you meet a track, go left. At a junction with a plethora of ELECTRICITY POLES (**1h45min**), take the track to the right, heading towards a house (CARZAVEC-CHIO), but without reaching it. Barking will herald your

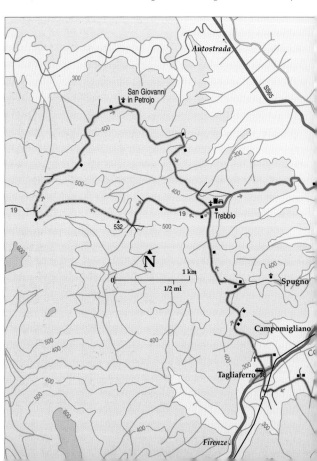

Mezzadria

The system of crop-sharing that has pervaded all aspects of Tuscan country life since medieval times, *mezzadria* has left a noticeable mark on the landscape. The system was an exchange. The landowner *(proprietario)* allowed a farmer and his family the use of a farm and its lands. In return the farmer, the *contadino*, gave the landowner half of everything the farm produced.

The landlord's estate was divided up into small units. Each farm *(podere)* was run autocratically by the eldest male. He organised his whole extended family, including the small children, to produce as much food as possible from the land. In fertile areas the family could live quite well off the produce. In poorer districts, such as those in the mountains, the peasants had barely a subsistence living and were often in debt to the owner.

The landlord was often quite a distant figure, though his permission had to be sought if a peasant's son wished to marry. This the landlord might refuse if he thought the farm was too small to support any progeny.

Initially the farmer was only responsible for providing a reasonable return to the landlord. But there was a day of reckoning at the end of every year and, if the landlord was not satisfied, he would ask the family to leave! More recently landlords employed estate managers *(fattora)* who lived at the *fattoria*. These men became notorious for cheating both the peasants and the landlords.

At one time two-thirds of Tuscany was organised under the *mezzadria* system. For centuries it provided a stable social framework that was generally thought to be fair and effective. But by the 18th century the system proved less effective. Both tenant and the (often absentee) landlord mistrusted each other.

Of course such systems are challenged by wars and technology. World War II especially took the men away from the farm and showed them a a different way of life. The wireless and the moped increased the families' knowledge of other ways of living. Young people started to reject the authority of their parents. They wanted to earn a wage and to have money to spend. They wanted to start married life in their own home. By the mid-1950s up to half of all Tuscan tenant farmers had left the land. It had taken less than a decade for the system to disintegrate. This was in spite of landowners making significant investments to improve the conditions on the farm, bringing gas and electricity to the farmhouse, and giving the farmer a greater share of the produce.

Map showing Scarperia, Sieve, Fortezza San Martino, Villa Adami, San Piero a Sieve, Borgo San Lorenzo, and contour lines at 300 and 400.

approach to the next house, where they breed pug dogs (**2h05min**). Here carry straight on along a dirt track between meadows. Where the main track bends left, veer right beside cherry trees and pass under the railway line (**2h15min**). Don't turn right just past the railway line, but turn right on the higher track you can see above. This takes you over the **River Carza** once more and you meet the old main road in **Tagliaferro**. Cross this road, take the track opposite, and cross the new main road by the bus stops. (Short walk 1 ends here.)

Follow the track ahead, starting up the hill and eventually joining a more important track, waymarked and well surfaced. Ignore all tracks to the right, until you arrive at the hamlet of **Trebbio** with its CASTLE (**3h**). Here the main walk continues to the left to make another circuit (Short walk 2). (Short walk 3 turns right on the unsealed road, for San Piero.)

After you have looked around the tiny hamlet of Trebbio with its castle, cypress-filled chapel courtyard, and Haflinger ponies grazing in the paddock, take the dirt track heading west uphill, following various waymarks: red and white for the CAI and yellow for the SOFT trekking route. At a junction by a WATER TROUGH (**3h20min**) go left, then turn right at a five-way junction. Beyond a summit (532m), a once-cobbled path descends along the ridge to a derelict farm on the left. Just around the bend from this house, on the right, two paths join the track: one descends from a large dead tree, the other, your ongoing path, drops steeply through bushes. Take care here, as this path is easy to miss (especially with the heavy growth of summer), and both the track and your path bear yellow waymarks. As you descend through the woods, ignore all the paths to the left.

The landscape opens out by an imposing old DAIRY FARM, sadly also derelict. Beyond the farm, stay with the track to the right (still following yellow waymarks), and head towards the church tower of San Giovanni in the distance. The track meets a major track just beyond **San Giovanni in Petrojo**

Church at San Piero a Sieve (above); San Giovanni in Petrojo (below left)

(**4h30min**), which you follow to the right (but first take a short detour to the church). Soon Trebbio's castle rises in the distance.

Back at **Trebbio** (**5h**), head downhill just past the chapel, along a winding unsealed road bordered by a magnificent line of cypress trees. When you meet the MAIN ROAD (**5h30min**)*, cross it and take the concrete road opposite (offset a short way to the right and waymarked in yellow). This leads to a house at a Y-junction. Take the lower track on the left, signposted 'FORTEZZA'. Within sight of the **Fortezza San Martino**, you come to a junction of tracks and a sign, 'LOCALITA FORTEZZA' (**5h45min**). To explore the fort (photograph page 15), go straight on and return to this junction later. Otherwise turn right. As you enter **San Piero** (**5h55min**), you will see the imposing VILLA ADAMI. Take the stone-paved road at the right of this villa, then any right turn will take you to the MAIN STREET (**6h**).

*If you want to swim, turn left on the main road and follow signs to the 'Mugello Verde' camp site (10min). You can buy a ticket at reception.

Cattle were the work-horses of the Tuscan farm, and the pride and joy of the man of the house. Rather as some men today love their cars and enjoy caring for them, so it was with the family ox or cow in rural Tuscany. In fact cows were more common than oxen. Oxen were used more often for heavier work such as hauling stone on sledges. But cows could be trained to pull a cart and a plough, and they provided meat and milk as well. The variety of cow used depended on the terrain as well as their main purpose — milk, meat or work. The most popular cattle were the Chianina, good for both work and meat.

As the cattle were so important to the peasants, they were provided with housing of almost the same quality as the family. The ground floor of the farmhouse would house animal stalls, often under or next to the kitchen or bedroom. Animals were rarely out of sight of some member of the family and were treated with great care and affection. Indeed in some areas dairy cows were always kept indoors; it was thought they would die if they ventured outside. To keep the animals warm in winter, the stalls had few openings and so were quite dark. (It was also believed that moonlight would turn the cows' eyes white.)

An old *contadina* told me that in her family the beasts were more highly valued than the women. They were harder to replace!

5 CIRCUIT FROM SANT'AGATA VIA THE APENNINE RIDGE

Distance/time: 19km/12mi; 5h

Grade: moderate, with a steady ascent of 700m/2300ft on farm tracks and woodland paths. Best suited for spring or autumn.

Equipment: as pages 137-138; also walking boots

How to get there and return: SITA 🚌 302 from Florence to/from Sant'Agata; journey time 1h10min. Or 🚗: park on the Scarperia road, by the bus stop (the 42.5km-point in Car tour 1)

Refreshments: bar at Sant'Agata

Short walk: Sant'Agata — Montepoli — Sant'Agata (8km/5mi; 2h 20min). Moderate, with an ascent of 430m/1400ft. Equipment and access as main walk. From the bus stop/car parking area follow the road towards Sant'Agata, but turn left before the village on the signposted road to Galliano. At the sign for Lumena (10min), turn right: this track is well waymarked (CAI 46 and two yellow dots for the Bologna-Florence route). Follow the track uphill and round the top of the valley, where it turns north (left). At a major junction (1h40min), leave the CAI and BO-FI route and turn right, by a wooden hut, to start the descent to Sant'Agata. Now follow different waymarks: the two yellow flashes of the SOFT 13 route. Pick up the main walk at the 4h20min-point.

Alternative walk: Giogo di Scarperia — Passo dell'Osteria Bruciata — Sant'Agata (19m/12mi; 5h). Moderate, with an ascent of 300m/1000ft, but note that the path is overgrown with scratchy bushes in places and there is one tricky climb near the edge of a steep drop. You must be sure-footed. This wonderful ridge walk is especially fine in summer. Equipment as main walk; access on SITA 🚌 303 from Florence or Scarperia to the Giogo Pass (Picnic 4); return by SITA 🚌 302 from Sant'Agata. Follow the CAI 00 northwest from the pass, to the ridge and along it. When you join the CAI 44 coming in from the left (2h15min), pick up the main walk at the 2h15min-point.

This walk climbs to the summit of the Apennines from the edge of the Mugello. After a long but pleasant climb (through beech woods in the latter stage), you achieve the summit ridge path with its magnificent views. Ahead are the retreating summits of the Apennine mountain chain. The huge fertile bowl of the Mugello is to the south, and to the north, in the direction of Bologna, are distant towns. The path is well waymarked and decorated with wild raspberries, sloe bushes and cyclamen. It passes through meadows covered with purple crocus and snowdrops in March and blue scillas in April. At the Passo Osteria

Bruciata (Burnt Inn Pass), the homeward journey begins, undulating through shade down an ancient trading route back to the charming village of Sant'Agata.

Start the walk on the main street of **Sant'Agata**. With the CHURCH and the BAR on the left, continue up the main street (VIA MONTACCIANICO). The route is well marked by two walking groups, so navigation is not a problem: just follow the red and white CAI 44 and the two yellow flashes of the SOFT 13 trekking route round the valley of the **Cornocchio River**.

Out of the village, the climb begins, at first along the road. Turn left, following signposting for 'CAVALLICO' (**15min**). This unsealed road takes you to a house tucked safely behind the hill to be out of the wind. Stay on this track which links occasional houses and a series of wooden crosses for the

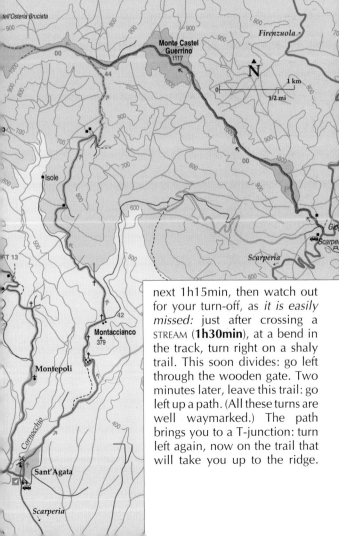

next 1h15min, then watch out for your turn-off, as *it is easily missed:* just after crossing a STREAM (**1h30min**), at a bend in the track, turn right on a shaly trail. This soon divides: go left through the wooden gate. Two minutes later, leave this trail: go left up a path. (All these turns are well waymarked.) The path brings you to a T-junction: turn left again, now on the trail that will take you up to the ridge.

CYCLAMEN

Seeing cyclamen growing wild in Italy is one of the joys of walking in the countryside. It seems so exotic and extravagant that such an elegant flower should be scattered carelessly in the debris of the Tuscan woodlands, even under brambly scrub. September to November is when the autumn-flowering species (*Cyclamen hederifolium*) appears to delight us, and March to May for the spring-flowering species (*Cyclamen repandum*). Both are members of the primrose family. Apart from the beauty of their swept-back delicate pink flowers, they have elegant leaves of variegated greens which appear after the first flowers. When flowering is over, the stems coyly curl up around the fruit until they are ready for the ants to disperse the sugar-coated seeds.

The Italian country name for this plant is *pan porcino* (pigs' bread'), as the tubers are a favourite food of the pig. The plants were valued by country people as a cure for earache and malaria. These cures were used during the Second World War, when other treatments were not available.

Ignore the many other woodland paths: follow the waymarked path, bearing gently left to round the top of the valley.

At the RIDGE (1022m/3352ft; **2h 15min**) turn left on the CAI 00. *(The Alternative walk joins here, from the right.)* Follow the crest to a picnic area and major junction of trails at the **Passo dell'Osteria Bruciata** (917m/3007ft; **3h**). The grisly legend of this *osteria* is that the innkeeper killed his rich guests, cooked them, and served them the next day for dinner! At the monument marking the pass, turn left towards Sant'Agata (CAI 46 *and* SOFT 13). The main, marked route is clear — usually a wide trail, but narrowing occasionally to a path. Important landmarks are: a THREE-WAY FORK (**3h25min**), where you take the middle route; a SHARP RIGHT TURN (**3h45min**), to skirt **Monte Linari**, passing a derelict farmhouse; a STAND OF PINES (**4h 10min**), beyond which you fork left.

When the WAYMARKS DIVERGE (**4h20min**), the main track drops to the right, with two yellow dots marking the Bologna to Firenze route. The trail to the left has the two yellow flashes of the SOFT 13. *(The Short walk joins here.)* Although *both* routes go to Sant'Agata, take the trail to the left, contouring initially, then dropping through woods and passing another ruin on the right. A rough trail then takes you past other ruined farms. After crossing a basin with a 'moonscape' of grey eroded cliffs, turn right at a TABERNACLE (**4h40min**). A tarred road comes underfoot at **Montepoli** (**4h 50min**) and takes you to a T-junction at **Sant'Agata** (**5h**). Turn left here on the old cobbled street, pass the church, and then go right, down to the BUS STOP and PARKING.

6 ALONG MICHELANGELO'S ROAD, FROM SERAVEZZA TOWARDS MONTE ALTISSIMO

See also photographs page 23

Distance/time 13km/8mi; 4h10min for motorists; 15km/9.3mi; 4h50min by public transport (in either case, allow extra time to visit the quarry)

Grade: moderate at first, with an initial climb of 300m/1000ft, then easy walking on mainly shady woodland tracks (overall ascent 440m/1450ft)

Equipment: as pages 137-138; also hiking boots

How to get there and return: 🚍 from Pisa to/from Pietrasanta, then CLAP 🚍 Q35 from Pietrasanta to/from Seravezza and follow notes for motorists to the start of the walk). Or 🚗: make for Seravezza direct from the A12 motorway. Otherwise, following Car tour 3, take the right turn at the first T-junction beyond Arni and continue to Seravezza (50km). Below Seravezza, cross the River Serra to the west bank and drive upstream. Beyond Rimagno there is an isolated pink house up on your left, by a weir. Park beyond it on the left, where the road opens out.

Refreshments: Bars and restaurants at Seravezza and Azzano

Short walk: Seravezza — quarry — Seravezza (8km/5mi; 2h45min). Grade, equipment and access as main walk. Follow the main walk to the chapel at the quarry (1h30min). Return either the way you came or by road (quiet except at the beginning and end of the working day).

This wonderful introduction to the Alpi Apuane gives you an insight into the magnificence of the area and the lifestyles of inhabitants past and present. The walk is set among low-level chestnut-covered slopes, but with awe-inspiring ridges above and fast-moving torrents below. The cobbled mule track followed for part of the way was reputedly built by Michelangelo to bring his precious white marble down from the mountain. For walkers, these ancient mule tracks today provide perfect links between the tiny villages with their steep labyrinthine streets the width of a donkey cart.

Start the walk across the road from the PARKING PLACE. Look for a flat-roofed building with the remains of a pulley system on top. Take the COBBLED TRAIL (grassy at the outset) winding left past an empty TABERNACLE and two old electricity pylons (one with a marking for Azzano). Though overgrown in places, the trail is easy to follow; it zigzags up the steep hillside, then veers to the left. Ignore all turnings to the right. When you reach a small CONCRETE BRIDGE BY A GATE, you are almost at Azzano. Beyond some houses, the trail turns right, but just go straight uphill, sometimes up steps, until you reach a second road (VIA MARTIRI DI LAVORO; **37min**). Turn right and follow the road past the restaurant, to the CHURCH and bar in the centre of **Azzano**.

Now take VIA PIANELLO (**50min**), a road between the church and a giant marble sculpture of corn on the cob! The road divides immediately: fork left and follow a narrow concrete road with CAI waymarks straight towards a wooden cross. Then go left along VIA VENEZIA (not waymarked). Ignore all paths crossing up and down from the village houses. After five minutes of gentle climbing, the road becomes gravel and flattens out a little. Ignore trails off to the right. Beyond a couple of houses you're on Michelangelo's old cobbled mule track. You pass a waterfall and the occasional cottage, before meeting a quarry road, white with marble dust (**1h20min**).

Follow the road up past a large hostel. Around the bend, there is a recently-built chapel dedicated to those killed at work (**1h30min**). There is also a stunning view of the amphitheatre of mountain peaks. Across the road, stone plaques set into a wall are engraved with poems extolling the magnificence of God and Nature compared to the vulnerability of man. Allow extra time if you carry on uphill to see the QUARRY itself and views of the sea, but stay away from the edges.

When the place has exhausted you, mentally or physically, retrace your steps to the CHURCH at **Azzano** (**2h35min**). Then take the little road opposite the front of the church, to the right of house number 83. Veer left to skirt a house on your right, then descend a mule track into the woods. At a clear T-junction, turn left to cross a stream. Now keep contouring; *do not descend steeply. Care is needed* at a few junctions. The first is just before a HOUSE (**2h47min**): take the right fork, to avoid the house. At a second junction, again fork right. At the third junction (just past a house; **2h55min**), go left. At the fourth junction, go left uphill to the 13th-century **Cappella di San Martino** (**3h**), with its 10th-century tower and rose window by Michelangelo.

Take the old stone trail below the church, past high stone walls and through old quarries. Descending through **Fabbiano**, turn right at the T-junction, go down steps, turn left on VIA BOTTEGHINO and walk into the piazza. The little alley continues below the piazza and leaves it in the far right-hand corner. Beyond the COMMUNAL LAUNDRY (**3h20min**), follow a mule track all the way down to **Rimagno** (**3h50min**). Turn right on the main road for 2km back to your car (**4h 10min**), or turn left to the BUS STOP at **Seravezza**, 1km away.

MARBLE FROM THE ALPI APUANE

This most useful type of rock was originally limestone built up from the skeletons of sea creatures. Pressure and/or heat caused the crystallisation of the limestone into marble. This crystallisation process needs to take place twice before marble's microscopic uniform sugar-like granules are formed. Mineral impurities, such as quartz and graphite incorporated into the white rock, give the colour to some marbles. But Carrara's famous white marble is 99% pure.

The Romans were serious users of the marble from this area. It was they who developed many of the extraction techniques used until recent times. A major problem was how to get the cut marble down the steep mountainsides. This the Romans solved by pioneering the *lizzatura* system, whereby the marble blocks were loaded onto wooden sledges. These they allowed to slide gently over greased rollers — tree trunks laid down specially-built sloping tracks. The speed of the sledge was controlled by men holding ropes from the sledge but anchored around stakes which were fixed deep in the ground. Though it was a very dangerous manoeuvre, the *lizzatura*

was still being used well into the 20th century. At the base of the mountains, the workers transferred the marble to bullock carts which transported it to the nearest navigable water. It was not until the end of the 19th century that things started to change. Steam power was able to provide continuous movement — for cutting marble, for instance. Thus a metal wire moving continuously, together with sand and water, replaced the saw, hammer and chisel. You can see the remains of this cutting system, lots of wheels and wire, in many abandoned quarries, and a model is to be found at the excellent Civic Museum of Marble in Carrara (see Car tour 3 on pages 20-23).

Top and left: quarries near Carrara (Car tour 3). Right: River Serra (top); marble scree below Monte Altissimo (middle); model cutting machine at the marble museum in Carrara (bottom)

7 CIRCUIT BELOW MONTE PROCINTO VIA THE ALTA MATANNA REFUGE

Distance/time: 7km/4.4mi; 4h15min

Grade: strenuous, with a shaded ascent of 500m/1650ft. You must be sure-footed and have a head for heights. The route is well trodden and signposted by the CAI. Suitable from spring through autumn.

Equipment: as pages 137-138; also walking boots and walking stick

How to get there and return: 🚗 only accessible by car. Take the A12 motorway towards Genova. Leave it at Pietrasanta, following signs for Seravezza and then Stazzema. Leave the Stazzema road after Mulina: turn right at a wide junction, following signposting for the Rifugio Forte di Marmi. Ignore any road on the left. Park after a sharp bend with a woodyard, near a notice board for the start of the walk. (Also accessible from Car tour 3: take the short-cut route after Arni.)

Refreshments: two refuges along the way, open daily from mid-June to mid-September, otherwise open only at weekends and holidays

This walk gets within touching distance of a great stone peak or two, rising like cathedral naves from the gentler mountain slopes. The route circles perhaps the single most dramatic feature of the Apuane — the 200m rock tower of Monte Procinto. Although some of these Dolomite-like peaks can appear somewhat intimidating, the walk itself at times seems like a gentle woodland stroll. At other times, however, there are hints of real mountaineering, as you follow steep and narrow paths close to precipitous edges. The reward is to achieve a ridge high enough to give you spectacular views of the Apuane peaks and, on a clear day, all the way to the Apennines and the sea.

Start the walk at the APUANE NOTICE BOARD (where you will find details of any closed paths). Walk up the mule track signposted to MONTE FORATO. As the trail bends to the left, you pass a *marginetta* — a STONE SHELTER WITH A SACRED IMAGE on the wall. *Marginette* are an important part of this mountain landscape, providing shelter and spiritual sustenance from the local saint, both very important in this alpine region. The trail soon divides: CAI 6 to the left, CAI 5 to the right. Turn right up the stony CAI 5 trail and steps, until you reach a *marginetta* next to the **Fonte della Grotta**. Here water gushes out of the mountain into a stone basin (**45min**).

Turn right here (CAI 5 *and* CAI 121), in five minutes coming to the **Rifugio Forte dei Marmi**, with dramatic views

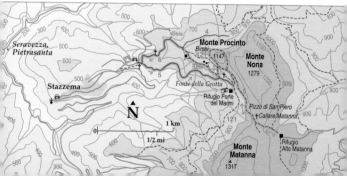

of Procinto from the terrace. From the refuge retrace your steps a short way, then turn right on the CAI 5 signposted for PROCINTO and MATANNA. As part of this path follows a fairly narrow ledge, the local CAI people have provided a *via ferrata* (**55min**), a safety wire attached securely into the rock. You need only use it as a handrail, but mountaineers scaling the sheer face of Monte Procinto use it to anchor their harnesses. Walk *past* the turn-off to Monte Procinto (you will return to this point later) and up to the **Pizzo** (peak) **di San Piero** (**1h 25min**). Here the path turn sharp right, hugging the slope beneath the great rock cliffs of Monte Nona. A pylon and WOODEN CROSS mark the pass called **Callare di Matanna** (1137m/3730ft; **1h30min**), between Nona and Matanna. You can turn back here, but the main walk continues to the refuge you can see below. Continue straight down the CAI 5, following the waymarks carefully. They lead you to the gate through the fence encircling the **Rifugio Alto Matanna** (**1h45min**). This setting is wonderful in late spring, when the surrounding pastures are full of flowers. Apart from a bar and restaurant, wild boar are kept here and (again, only in late spring), you may well see some of their young.

After a break, return the way you came as far as the PATH TO MONTE PROCINTO (**2h25min**). Turn right uphill here, to reach a 40-minute circuit path round the base of Procinto's massive stone stub. Follow the path up to and under the massive overhang, then descend to a bridge over a gully. From there turn right to begin the circuit. Once on the west side of the peak, watch for a path leading off right to a viewpoint over the 'Bimbi' (Children) of Procinto — sheer-sided upthrusts much loved by rock-climbers. When the circuit is almost complete, you can see the *via ferrata* to the summit (only suitable for properly-equipped mountaineers).

Having completed the circuit, return to the main path and follow it back down to the *fonte* (**3h20min**). Your return path is the CAI 5BIS that passes in front of the spring. Ignore the CAI 121, which follows a higher route to the right. After passing a strange BEEHIVE-SHAPED STONE BUILDING, when you come to a fork take the lower, left-hand path. This passes two deserted houses, the first of which has a *burraia* by its side (see page 106). Watch for your path forking sharply right; it

Left: model of a chestnut-drying house, in the Museum of Peasant Life at Palazzuolo (Car tour 1)

The tree is thought to have been brought from the Orient in Roman times and was widely planted in Italy, where it thrives well. It can grow to over 30 metres high (100ft) and has recognisable long green leaves with deeply-serrated edges. They were popular with mountain people and hill farmers, as the trees grow quickly and need little care. Not only do they produce useful food and wood but, with the right conditions around the roots, many edible fungi will grow. The wild trees growing on higher slopes produce *castagne*, the much smaller nuts.

SWEET CHESTNUTS

The sweet chestnut, *Castanea sativa*, has been an important part of the rural economy for hundreds of years. The trees grow prolifically on the slopes of Tuscan mountains at altitudes of 300 to 1000m. They like acid soil and lots of sun — and as the summer sun fades the leaves turn from dark green to lemon yellow and then to brown.

It is easiest to recognise the sweet chestnut by its flowers in early summer and by its fruit in autumn. The flowers are conspicuous bunches of fluffy, creamy-yellow catkins — the female flowers. (The male catkins are less showy.) The fruits are unmistakeable: small prickled green balls, perfect for protecting the nuts inside. The fruits start to fall in autumn. This event energises many city-dwellers, who leave their televisions and head for the hills, plastic collecting-bags in their glove-covered hands. Country people usually collect chestnuts when they are mature (after their prickly shells open and they lie on the ground). September 20th is traditionally the beginning of the harvest.

The use made of the nuts depends largely on their size. The largest nuts, called *marrone fiorentine*, are either boiled or roasted over the fire in a special perforated pan with a very long handle, then just eaten. Smaller nuts are dried whole, to be reconstituted by soaking in water. The least good nuts are ground into chestnut flour and made into cakes such as the *baldino di castagno* (chestnut flour mixed with water into a dough, then baked, well-greased with olive oil and flavoured with rosemary). Chestnut flour helped many Italians survive World War II, when no other food was available. Today, in the winter, the hot chestnut seller is still very much a part of the city centre scene in Florence.

---

has a short *via ferrata* (**3h30min**) to help you up the slope.

The gate of a lived-in mountain COTTAGE marks the point where the path bends sharp right, to descend beside a fence. When you come to a trail, follow it to the left. This trail soon divides: keep left on the CAI 5BIS, the higher of the two forks. At the next junction, go left again down steps (**3h50min**). This is the CAI 6 signposted to STAZZEMA, a superbly-cobbled mule track. Descends steeply back to a T-junction with the CAI 5 and turn right, back to the NOTICE BOARD (**4h15min**).

8 CIRCUIT FROM FOCIOMBOLI VIA FAVILLA AND THE FOCE DI MOSCETA

Distance/time: 9km/5.6mi; 3h10min (plus any time taken to reach Fociomboli from your parking place: see 'How to get there')

Grade: fairly strenuous, with a protracted climb of 500m/1650ft; otherwise along undulating woodland paths. Plenty of shade, so suitable all year round, except during winter. *Do* get local advice about weather conditions before setting off approaching the winter months.

Equipment: as pages 137-138; also walking boots, stick and other mountain essentials

How to get there and return: 🚗 only accessible by car. If following Car tour 3, take the short-cut route beyond Arni. Otherwise, take the A12 motorway towards Genova. Leave it at Pietrasanta, following signs for Seravezza and then Stazzema. Where the Stazzema road turns off to the right, continue up the Castelnuovo road, via Levigliani. Turn off right to Passo Croce and park along the quarry road to the summit of Monte Corchia (ignoring the quarry track off to the right). The road is passable for 1.5km, but it is best to park before the tarmac ends and continue to Fociomboli on foot.

Refreshments: only at the Rifugio del Freo (open weekends all year round and daily from mid-June to mid-September)

Short walk: Fociomboli — Puntato — Fociomboli (8km/5mi; 2h40min). Fairly easy, with an ascent of 300m/1000ft. Equipment and access as main walk. Follow the main walk to the 5min-point. Don't turn left down the CAI 11, but continue on a good track all the way to the goods cable lift and houses above Puntato (30min). Turn left just past a house with an outdoor oven, and follow the path in a bend to the left, crossing a stream. Walk down through the pasture on the left bank until you meet the CAI 11, a stone-laid mule track which you follow left back to Fociomboli. (But first turn right to visit the little church at Puntato.)

Longer walk: Isola Santa — Favilla — Foce di Mosceta — Isola Santa (13km/8mi; 5h). Very strenuous, with an overall ascent of 1000m/3300ft. Follow Car tour 3 to Isola Santa (the 32km-point). Park in the lay-by above the restaurant. Walk downhill along the road as far as the dam wall, where you pick up the CAI 9: cross the dam wall, turn right below the house, then climb to Favilla, ignoring a waymarked path to the left 25min uphill from the dam. Pick up the main walk at the 1h05min-point, follow it to Fociomboli, then use the notes from the start back to Favilla and walk back down the CAI 9.

Here, as in so many parts of Tuscany, the natural beauty of the landscape is enhanced by man-made structures left behind by past inhabitants. The scenery is stunning: great limestone mountaintops crown steep beech-covered slopes and gentle alpine pastures, home to a dazzling array of spring wild flowers. Mountain villages on 1000m-high ridges fill one with awe, as do the cobbled tracks over precipitous passes. No wonder they built stone shelters (*marginette*) along these ancient routes, each *marginetta* containing an image of a helpful saint: in winter the wayfarers of centuries past needed all the help they could get! Quarries at over 1500m are pretty impressive too: while they scar the landscape, they are a monumental testament to the men who

excavated them without great diesel-powered machines.

From wherever you park your car, continue along the QUARRY ROAD below the western wall of Monte Corchia, surrounded by an array of other peaks. You are walking at 1200m/3900ft, with far-reaching views. Ignore the CAI 129 descending to the left but, not much further along, where the unsealed road becomes very rough, you will see a track on the left. This area is **Fociomboli**, the pass between Monte Corchia and Monte Freddone, and the **walk timings begin here**. Descend this track to the second *marginetta* (**5min**), which has two rooms. Opposite is the well-marked CAI 11: follow this cobbled mule track downhill to the left. *(But for the Short walk, go right.)* You pass to the left of a large grassy *cirque,* once a lake formed in the course of the last glaciation. Now it is a collecting point for water for the stream, the **Canale delle Febbre**, that feeds the reservoir at Isola Santa. Stay on the left bank of the stream until you come to a CONCRETE HUT (**20min**). Cross the stream here and continue downhill beside the stream to pastures littered with cowslips (in May) and abandoned shepherds' huts. This is **Puntato**, where the trail veers right and, lined with beech trees, continues to a tiny CHURCH (**35min**). *(From the church the Short walk returns along the CAI 11 to Fociomboli.)*

Turn right in front of the church, along another tree-lined trail (still the CAI 11). Trees were probably planted in this way to protect the mule track from erosion. The trail mostly contours now, heading for Favilla, where the church tower is visible from time to time. Ignore both the CAI 128 to the right and a path to the left, then cross a STREAM (**50min**).

This relaxing section of the hike ends when you meet a track rising from the left. Turn right uphill here, to the deserted village of **Favilla** (**1h05min**). *(The Longer walk joins here.)* At least the church has been restored, and the large wooden table outside it makes a good lunch spot (the village fountain is also still working, if your water bottle needs a refill). Before leaving Favilla, take the path on the far side of the church up the ridge to the walled CEMETERY, the last resting place of these toughest of people and used at least until 1953. More forsaken farms sit proudly on the ridge, and a cherry orchard survives, sitting poignantly on the slope below.

Leaving the church, start off to the left of the fountain, following a magnificent stone-laid trail built for the charcoal-makers, now the CAI 9. Head uphill through beech woods. At a junction, go left, down to a STREAM (**1h25min**). The old bridge is long gone, but the stone ramp from it remains. It is not hard to imagine loaded donkeys toiling up this steep trail. The route crosses a couple of stream beds descending in gullies — even in early summer they may still be filled with snow and difficult to cross.

When the vegetation

CHARCOAL-MAKING

If country folk were angry with ungrateful offspring they often said, 'Well if you don't like it here, go and make charcoal', for charcoal-making was considered the worst possible job. It was dirty, hard, lonely work carried out in the depths of mountain forests.

The job of the charcoal-burners was to slowly 'cook' sticks of wood in huge bonfires to remove their moisture. For centuries charcoal was a very important fuel for housewives' ovens and blacksmiths' fires. The charcoal-burner made his bonfires on flat 'piazzas' in the mountains (see above). When the wood-pile was two to three metres high, he surrounded it with green brushwood and a low wall of sods, then covered the whole lot with soil. To control the speed of burning he left several air holes that he could open and close.

When the fire reached a temperature of 300-400°C, the real drying out began. It could take as long as 72 hours for the drying-out, during which time the *carbonaio* tended the fire constantly. A change in the colour of the smoke indicated that the process was over. The *carbonaio* left the pile to cool for about five days. Finally he sorted the charcoal by size, sacked it and sent it down the mountain by mule.

Top: deserted village of Favilla (left); crossing snow-slopes and 'snow rivers' on the ascent to the Foce di Mosceta (right and far right); bottom: church at Isola Santa (Car tour 3 and Longer walk 8); gnarled old chestnut tree

changes, you will know that you are almost at the **Foce di Mosceta**. On this shoulder the landscape is moor-like and marshy, with pines instead of beech trees. At the T-junction turn right over a wooden bridge to the red **Rifugio del Freo** (**1h55min**).

The signposted CAI 129 beyond the refuge is your ongoing route below the summit of **Monte Corchia**, famous for the series of pot-holes beneath it. The rough, rocky climb veers to the right through heather, wimberry and juniper. At a summit of sorts, the path starts to drop once more through beech woods. This was another charcoal-makers' route, and you pass several flattened areas ('piazzas'; see photograph page 71) where they would have built their 'bonfires'. Watch out for your SHARP LEFT TURN-OFF (**2h25min**), zigzagging up to the ridge. Once on the crest, the CAI 129 veers to the left for a while. During the next wooded stretch, ignore a path descending to the right. Later, when the trail divides, fork left: this takes you to a QUARRY TRACK (**3h05min**). Turn right back to **Fociomboli** (**3h10min**), then retrace your steps back to your CAR.

Walk 9: sheep at Guzzano (left) and winter woodlands at Bagni di Lucca

9 BAGNI DI LUCCA CIRCUIT

See photographs opposite, below

Distance/time: 17km/10.6mi; 4h25min

Grade: moderate-strenuous, with an ascent of 350m/1150ft. There is a stream to ford, but this is only a problem after several weeks of rain.

Equipment: as pages 137-138; also long trousers, walking boots

How to get there and return: Lazzi 🚌 from Lucca to/from Bagni di Lucca Villa; journey time 50min. Follow instructions for motorists to get to the start of the walk, adding 20min each way. Or 🚗: Follow signs for Bagni di Lucca from the 69km-point on Car tour 3, or drive direct from Lucca (27km). Once on the north bank of the Lima River, continue upstream to the part of town called La Villa. Pass the main piazza and the Hotel Roma, and take the second left turn, signposted to Montefegatesi. Then turn right towards Orridorio di Botri and San Gemignano. Five minutes up the road, you come to the stone church at Bagnicaldi: turn right directly opposite it, and park in that street.

Refreshments: bars at San Gemignano and San Cassiano

Short walks: The main walk is a figure-of-eight; each circuit can be done separately.

1 Bagnicaldi — San Gemignano — Bagnicaldi (9.5km/6mi; 3h). Grade, equipment and access as main walk. Follow the main walk to San Gemignano (1h35min). From the bar, turn left on the main road and pick up the notes again at the 3h05min-point, to return to your car.

2 San Gemignano — San Cassiano — San Gemignano (7km/4.5mi; 1h30min). Fairly easy, with an ascent of 100m/330ft. There is a stream to ford (only a problem after several weeks of rain). Equipment as main walk. Access by 🚗: follow directions for motorists above, but continue to San Gemignano and park. From the bar in the village, pick up the notes at the 1h35min-point and follow them to the 3h05min-point.

If you would like a mountain walking experience without having to motor along tortuous roads or do too much climbing, this is the walk for you. Bagno di Lucca is a popular spa town on the southernmost end of the Garfagnana. This walk takes you from the town up into the foothills of high mountains, including Tre Potenze and Rondinaio in the northwest Apennines. There are wonderful panoramas of mountain peaks, including those of the Alpi Apuane to the west. You follow ancient mule tracks which join isolated hamlets to cemeteries, churches and villages. Whether you do a short circuit or the main walk (a good full day's outing), space, air and fine scenery are your constant companions.

Start the walk on VIA DEL CIMITERO in **Bagnicaldi**, the road opposite the CHURCH: walk to the CEMETERY. Cross the parking area outside the cemetery gate and find the trail ahead, dropping down to the valley. Within minutes, when you meet the stream, take the trail down its right-hand bank. Turn left at the road (VIA CAMPIGLIA), skirting above the clear waters of the **River Lima**. You may spot some BLUE SHOE-SHAPED WAYMARKS. These are not regular enough to be relied on, but are reassurance that you are on the right route.

The road becomes a trail before meeting a second road

that crosses a BRIDGE (**15min**). Immediately after crossing the bridge, leave the road: take the gravel track on the left, to a house. Beyond the house turn right through bamboo, then skirt the upper edge of the bamboo, veering left and beginning to climb steeply up through woods. This old mule track is better in winter, when the trees are bare and the landscape exposed. In summer it is very overgrown with brambles, but they are a good reason to take your time as you zigzag almost directly up the left side of the hill. Suddenly you are at **Guzzano** (**1h**), the first of the mountain villages.

Walk left through this isolated collection of austere mountain houses. At the Y-junction by a CHAPEL, turn right up the road past the communal taps, to a little PIAZZA (**1h05min**), then cross the end of it on a cobbled track. Continue uphill to the right, past houses 132 and 133. Follow this mule-track below the ridge, but turn right at a V in the ridge, to pass a TABERNACLE and walk on into the parish of **Controne** (**1h15min**). From the church, set on a shoulder, there are new views up to the mountains in the north. The route continues along the right-hand wall of the church, goes left round the back of it, and then veers off to the right. This old route passes Controne's impressive stone COMMUNAL WATER SOURCE, with basins, tap, and laundry area. On the outskirts of **San Gemignano**, turn left to the CHURCH (**1h35min**) in the main street. The bar is straight ahead. (*Short walk 1 returns to Bagnicaldi from here, by picking up the notes at the 3h05min-point, and Short walk 2 joins here.*)

From the bar retrace your steps a short way, then go left down the track between houses 101 and 91. This is a wonderful old cobbled track, though rather slippery with moss. Follow it in a curve to the left, to cross a stream on a wooden bridge. On the far side you pass a METAL PYLON WAY-MARKED WITH AN ORANGE SHOE. Stay on the main trail, walking parallel with the valley, eventually curving round to the left. At the hamlet of **Vetteglia**, turn left on a cart track that passes through an orchard by a tiny CHAPEL with two bells (**1h50min**). Then go left at a T-junction, to begin your descent into a second valley, beyond which is a village with a distinctive church. As you drop into this valley, keep on the main track (the one that is obviously used by vehicles). When this track bends to the right, take a PATH (**2h02min**) off to the left, going straight downhill and crossing a tiny stream bed almost immediately. As this path can be indistinct in places, head towards the sound of the river. Soon you will meet a more obvious path: follow this to the left.

This path widens out and leads to the confluence of two streams. Cross the water (usually quite shallow), and head

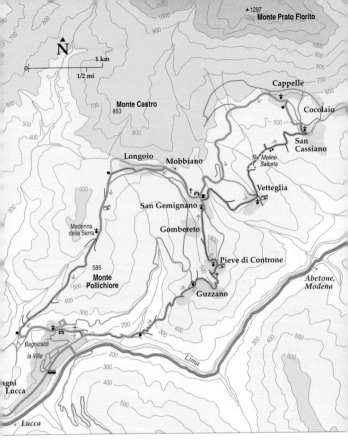

up the right-hand stream bed. Walk to the right of an ABAN-DONED MILL, still with its grinding wheels intact. Beyond the mill, take a track to the right, passing two houses. When you reach a junction, go left uphill to the CHURCH at **San Cassiano** **(2h30min)**. Almost immediately after tar comes under foot, turn left uphill on the church path. As you pass by the front of the church, have a look at the intricate carving on the façade, and the strange design of the whole building. It is almost as if they built the nave intending to demolish the tower, but hadn't the courage to actually do it.

At the three-way junction ahead, take the lower road to the left (by the pizzeria). This ends at a house, from where a short track takes you back up to the main road. Turn left on the road, past a CHAPEL and BUS STOP, with a steep-sided lime-stone mountain towering above. Its name is Monte Prato Fiorito (Flowering Field Mountain). This stretch of road-walking (about 3km) gives you time to relax until you reach **San Gemignano** again **(3h05min)**. Don't go left into the village, but keep round to the right, to the SHOP AND POST BOX. Take the track across the road from the post box; it is lined

Hunters are a powerful lobby group in Italy. They have effectively protected their sport from pressure from conservationists at home and abroad.

Not very long ago, most Italians were living off the land. The Second World War tolled the final death knell of a rural way of life that had lasted for centuries.

It is not surprising then that hunting, which had for centuries provided an important source of food, is considered a right of the working man by the majority of Italians.

In Italy it is legal to shoot all wild birds and animals except birds of prey, small insectivores, herons, woodpeckers and certain other protected species. This means that song birds are shot, as are 11 varieties of birds and animals protected in the rest of Europe, and 19 migratory species, 11 of which are protected internationally. Sixty per cent of Italy's wild vertebrates are in danger of extinction.

The hunting season is generally from the third Sunday in September to January 31st, excluding Tuesdays and Thursdays. Hunters can roam across private land unless the land is fenced in and marked 'no hunting'.

I have always found hunters careful and courteous. Indeed it is they that have kept the land accessible for walkers, by lobbying for open access and by using the footpaths.

If you hear shots, stay on the path and make lots of noise, so they know you are around.

with acacia trees; in June, their flowers perfume the air with the essence of Tuscany in summer. The track contours past some hamlets below Monte Castro. (There are various tracks here; they all meet up later, but keep to the contour, by the houses.) Beyond **Mobbiano**, take the lower unsealed road to **Longoio** (**3h20min**), where you meet a road and CAR PARK. Keep right here, up to the houses, one of which has a bridge-like arch. A mule track on the right takes you up and around the back of the houses (including numbers 29 and 2). Continue to a solitary white house (number 3), where you fork left. At the next junction, go straight ahead. At the third junction, where there is a plethora of red waymarks on the trees, keep left. This track leads to the tiny chapel of **Madonna della Serra** (**3h40min**), in the woods.

Beyond the chapel, at a three-way fork, take the middle route, descending to the left of a steep, thickly-wooded valley. A little over 1km along, ignore a way-marked route up to the left. About 500m/yds further on, the trail turns down to the right. Keep straight ahead here on a path (**4h05min**), descending steeply to a track. Turn left on the track and, on coming to a house, fork left. Then go left again on the road, back down to the CHURCH in **Bagnicaldi** (**4h25min**).

10 MONTE FALCO, MONTE FALTERONA AND THE SOURCE OF THE ARNO

Distance/time: 13km/8mi; 4h15min

Grade: moderate, but with two ascents, each about 300m/1000ft. Clear, well-waymarked paths. The route is high and shady, suitable for most of the year, except at the height of winter (approaching winter, you need to take local weather advice, as the high mountains have a microclimate all their own).

Equipment: as pages 137-138; also walking boots

How to get there and return: 🚗 only accessible by car. Leave Car tour 4 at the 48km-point: turn left on the SS310 for Stia. Take the right turn in Stia for the Passo della Calla, an attractive but winding road. Park at the car park at the pass.

Refreshments: none en route

Short walks

1 Monte Falco and Monte Falterona (9km/5.5mi; 3h15min). Moderate, with an ascent of 300m/1000ft; equipment and access as main walk. Follow the main walk to the 1h35min-point, then turn right off the trail onto a footpath (still the CAI 00), to Monte Falterona. Return the way you came.

2 Piancancelli — Monte Falco — Piancancelli (5km/3mi; 1h40min). Easy-moderate, with an ascent of 200m/650ft. Equipment as main walk. Access by 🚗: drive to Passo della Calla as for the main walk, but from there continue on the unsealed road to the left. Pass the restaurant/bar Capanna and park at the pass of Piancancelli. From here follow the CAI 00 signposted to Monte Falco. Picnic in the meadow on the ridge or continue on the CAI 00 to Monte Falterona. Return the same way.

This high-level, shady walk is very enjoyable on a hot day — even in August. This area, in the Alpe di San Benedetto, is also a ski resort. The walk has spectacular views, especially to the north — over the strange desert-like mountain landscape of the neighbouring Emilia Romagna region. Although there is plenty of climbing (two of the highest peaks in the area are climbed), there are also pleasant strolls through magical beech woods. Seeing the source of the Arno River with its plaque bearing a quotation from Dante is also fun … even if the spring is without water!

Start the walk by the REFUGE in front of the car park at the

On the summit of Monte Falterona

HELLEBORES

Several varieties of *Helleborus* grow in the Tuscan woodlands up to about 1000m/3000ft.

Helleborus foetidus — called the 'stinking hellebore' because of the nasty smell produced when it is crushed — is the tallest and most common, the plants rising boldly amid the dead winter foliage. Their boldness does not extend to their drooping flowerheads, however, which are very pale in colour (usually faint green to white). Even the very showiest of the species can only boast a brown tinge at the edges of its petals.

The 'Christmas rose' types of hellebore are also common in the winter woods. They are shorter, stockier plants, with one to three larger flowers on a stem. The flowers have brave open faces of a most delicate green which bend shyly towards the earth. It is as if their beauty is almost too much for the drab winter landscape. To me these are very precious plants, surviving even snow, to maintain a living presence through the winter months. In the ancient language of flowers however, they were the symbol of false accusations. How sad!

All hellebores are poisonous, although in Italy they were once used as a (very dangerous) remedy for worms in children.

The way their seeds are spread is novel. Snails are attracted to an oily substance surrounding the seeds. When they approach, the seeds attach themselves to the snail. The snail then wanders off, later dropping the seeds in another area.

Passo della Calla. Follow the well-waymarked CAI 00 up towards Monte Falco. The only tricky section is after a STONE REFUGE (**25min**), where the path bears left into an open area (Picnic 10, part of a ski run). Follow the signs guiding you diagonally left and uphill across the meadow. The path meets a track at a T-junction: turn right along the ridge, past stunted beech trees and pines, almost 'bonsaied' by the wind. The track skirts a fenced off area of MASTS (**55min**), before continuing up to the SUMMIT of **Monte Falco** (1658m/5438ft; **1h20min**). Just beyond the summit post there is a rock ledge overlooking the rest of the world — a perfect spot for picnicking and contemplation.

Moving on, continue along the CAI 00, below the ridge. When you

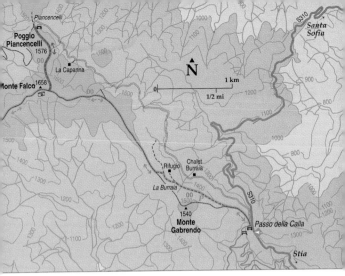

come to a fork where the CAI 00 turns right up to Monte Falterona (**1h35min**), keep left on the main trail (now CAI 4). *(But for Short walk 1, turn right on the CAI 00.)* At the signposted junction, turn right down the CAI 3 for 'Capo d'Arno' (**1h40min**). At the bottom of this steep wooded path, follow the signs to the **Capo d'Arno** (**1h 55min**), a little trickle of clear water that is start of the Arno River — so huge, grey and muddy when it flows through Florence in winter.

Walk ahead past the source, to take a forest track heading up to the right towards Le Crocicchie. Ignore the first sign you pass on the right (indicating another path up to Monte Falterona; **2h05min**); take the second path (signposted to Le Crocicchie; **2h15min**).

Le Crocicchie (**2h20min**), the saddle, is the far point of this walk. A tough but interesting climb lies ahead. Turn right here, back onto the CAI 00. The path *almost* hugs the sheer drop to the left, but is not close enough to be frightening; you will be too busy concentrating on the rocky footpath and following the red and white markings as they weave through the trees. At one clearing there is a tiny shrine hanging over the edge of the cliff.

The sight of the wooden cross is very welcome as you achieve the summit of **Monte Falterona** (1654m/5425ft; **2h 45min**). Carry straight on past the cross, but veer to the left, heading northeast, down the ridge. After another stunning viewpoint, the path descends into the woods and joins the wide CAI 4 trail (**2h55min**). Turn left here to retrace your steps back to **Monte Falco** and the car park (**4h15min**).

11 CIRCUIT FROM THE ABBEY AT VALLOMBROSA VIA MONTE SECCHIETA

Distance/time: 11km/6.9mi; 3h10min

Grade: moderate, with a climb of 500m/1650ft at the outset, followed by an easy descent along shady well-marked trails. Suitable all year round, except in deepest winter and at the very height of summer.

Equipment: as pages 137-138; also walking boots

How to get there and return: SITA 🚌 321 from Florence to/from Vallombrosa (it is necessary to change buses at Pontassieve); journey time 1h30min. Or 🚗: drive to the abbey at Vallombrosa (the 24km-point on Car tour 4); park at the side of the building, next to the fish ponds.

Refreshments: bar and restaurant at Vallombrosa, bar at Monte Secchieta

Short walks

1 Monte Secchieta — Croce al Cardeto — La Macinaia — Monte Secchieta (7km/4.3mi; 2h). Quite easy, with an ascent of 150m/500ft. Equipment as main walk. Access by 🚗: park at the summit of Monte Secchieta (detour beyond Vallombrosa, the 24km-point in Car tour 4). Follow the main walk from the 1h06min-point to the 2h-point, then turn right up the track (CAI 12), back to your car at the summit.

2 Vallombrosa — Monte Secchieta — La Macinaia — Vallombrosa (6.5km/4mi; 2h30min). Grade, equipment and access as main walk. Follow the main walk to Monte Secchieta and continue past the bar for 5min. Then take the first track on the right (CAI 12). Pick up the main walk again just after the 2h-point, at the cottage called La Macinaia.

3 Vallombrosa — Fonte Santa Caterina — CAI 12 — Bocca del Lupo — Vallombrosa (4km/2.5mi; 1h). Easy; equipment as pages 137-138; access as main walk. From the abbey, follow the main road towards Saltino. Pick up the signposted CAI 12 at the Fonte Santa Caterina. Keep left at a fork and, when you reach a junction, Bocca del Lupo, turn left down the CAI 11, back to the abbey.

The mountains of the Pratomagno are enclosed by the great loop of the River Arno. High, wooded, and running with water, they provide the perfect summer cooling-off spot for the inhabitants of the busy Valdarno valley to the west. The abbey of Vallombrosa and the nearby village of Saltino are much loved by the local people in July and August, but neglected for the rest of the year. It is indeed good summer

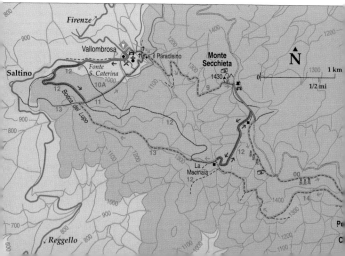

Double cross near Saltino and chestnut trees at the rocky promontory reached in 1h40min, with the snow-capped main ridge of the Pratomagno in the background

walking country, when the rest of Tuscany is frying, and wonderful in winter, too, when more views are exposed and the land is partially covered in snow. This is an area with ample snowfall, so if you plan to walk in winter, take local advice before setting out and be properly equipped.

Start the walk at the car park by the rectangular FISH POND next to the ABBEY at **Vallombrosa**. Here you will find the start of the CAI 9, the beginning of the climb. The CHURCH is on your right and a stream on the left. Cross the bridge by the waterfall, and head up a cobbled path stepping its way past three small chapels to the hermitage above. Follow this path all the way to the road. The hermitage, **Il Paradisino**, will be on your right (**15min**).

Cross the road and continue straight uphill, climbing a rather rough, stony path veering to the left. It heads round the side of the valley, then descends towards two streams. Before the trail meets the streams, take a steep path on your left, the well-waymarked CAI 9 towards Secchieta (**30min**).

After an initial climb, the path contours round the valley, crossing TWO STREAMS (**45min**). Watch for the waymarks, as there are many other forest paths. The route turns left in front of rocks blocking the trail ahead, and later climbs the shoulder of the hill. One more SHARP TURN TO THE RIGHT (**1h**) takes you further uphill — hard work, but the path is through beech trees which are always a joy.

The end of the climb brings you to an array of masts along the SUMMIT RIDGE of **Monte Secchieta** (1450m/ 4756ft; **1h06min**). While they intrude on the beauty of the landscape, there *are* some rewards for all your effort — the view and a bar across the road. The bar staff will let you eat your packed lunch inside if you buy a drink — most welcome in winter.

From the summit turn right on the wide unsealed road, leading to more ubiquitous masts. *(Short walk 1 starts here.)* Continue past the start of the CAI 12 five minutes past the bar. *(But for Short walk 2, turn right down this track.)* After passing a fenced-off property, turn off right on the CAI 00, ascending the ridge, just

Croce al Cardeto

81

WILD BOAR

All you are likely to see of this animal are its hoofprints along a muddy path, unless of course you go to a restaurant specialising in game (look for *cinghiale* on the menu).

Wild boar are nocturnal and shy, but can be aggressive if they feel their young are being threatened. Because of their large size (up to 175 kg), the ridge of thick fur along their backs, and their small tusks, they do look quite fierce. In much of Tuscany the numbers of native wild boar declined, so local hunters introduced a Hungarian boar which breeds prolifically. Now this variety inhabits the Tuscan woodlands, although it can adapt to many types of environment.

As they have no predators, except the human kind, they have increased greatly in numbers, doing much damage in farming areas.

This salumeria *in Greve specialises in wild boar*

below the masts. There are vast views in every direction. The Arno Valley is on both sides and, if it is high summer, this area is covered with wild raspberries in full fruit. After the last tall mast, follow the path down left to the road at the pass of **Croce al Cardeto** (**1h30min**). Another, smaller mast seen ahead marks the summit of Poggio alla Cesta at 1446m/4742ft. It's just a five-minute walk away (CAI 00), if you want to make this detour.

The main walk turns down from Croce al Cardeto, however, heading right on the CAI 14 towards Vallombrosa (signposted). The wide trail soon ends, but the route continues as a narrow path heading left. It drops steeply into the trees, then veers to the right. Take care to follow the red waymarks carefully through the trees, until you arrive at a ROCKY PROMONTORY (**1h 40min**) overlooking the valley. Turn right and follow the path around the bowl of the valley.

At a junction (**2h**) take the trail up to the right, to a cottage (LA MACINAIA). Turn left here on the CAI 12, a track descending from Monte Secchiata. *(Short walk 1 turns right uphill on this track, and Short walk 2 rejoins the main walk here.)* Ignore a turning to the left but, at the next junction, turn left uphill on the CAI 13 (**2h20min**). This lovely trail is easy walking, with spectacular views of wooded ridges and south over the Arno Valley.

This trail ends at a signposted junction, **Bocca del Lupo (2h50min)**.* Turn right on the CAI 11. You cross a mountain road and a tarred road and come to the back of the ABBEY at **Vallombrosa (3h10min)**.

*If you would like to see Saltino or buy an ice-cream, continue on CAI 13 from here to the road. Then turn right past holiday homes and walk on to Vallombrosa, along a woodland path below the road.

12 CIRCUIT FROM CASPRI VIA MONTE COCOLLO AND POGGIO MONTRAGO

Distance/time: 16km/10mi; 4h30min

Grade: moderate, with two climbs, each of about 300m/1000ft, but otherwise fairly level walking. There is very little shade along the way, so this walk is not suitable in summer. Navigation is easy.

Equipment: as pages 137-138

How to get there and return: 🚗 best reached by car. Leave Castelfranco di Sopra (the 112km-point on Car tour 4; 10min from the Valdarno exit on the A1 motorway) on the road to Pian di Scò, then turn right just outside town, following signposting to Caspri. Park at the junction with the second road on the left (again signposted to Caspri), on the left, by the communal rubbish bins. The walk is also accessible by ALA 🚐 from Arezzo to/from Castelfranco; for timetables telephone 0575-984140.

Refreshments: none en route

Short walks

1 Casa La Quercia al Nibbio — Monte Cocollo — Casa La Quercia al Nibbio (8km/5mi; 2h20min). Moderate, with an ascent of 200m/650ft. Equipment as pages 137-138. Access: follow the directions for the main walk, but ignore the parking at the second junction. Instead continue up to the right for 1.5km, to a house on the right with an imposing gate and CAI waymarks on the wall. Park on the left here. Join the main walk at the 25min-point. At the 1h10min-point take the CAI 33 down to the right. A few minutes later you join the CAI 35, on the right. Follow this clear well-marked track for 30min, *paying careful attention at two points.* The first point of potential confusion comes up six to seven minutes after you join the CAI 35 (1h20min): here you will be on a wide, flat area, and you will see a track running parallel with the track you are on, to the right: move over to this second track now. It narrows to a waymarked path and descends to the right. The second place where you might go wrong comes up ten minutes later (1h30min), when you meet a level path coming from the left. Go left here (if you come to a house you have missed your turn) and, two minutes later, turn right on a shady path. Follow the waymarks carefully as you descend, veering to the right. When you reach a track (1h37min), turn left and continue to an unsealed road by two houses. Turn right here, to round the hill, then take the second right turn, to climb back to Odina. Turn left past the chapel, retracing the CAI 33 back down to your car.

2 Castelfranco — Pulicciano — Galligiano — Caspi — Castelfranco (10km/6.3mi; 2h30min). Easy-moderate, with an ascent of 250m/820ft; not suitable on a hot day. Equipment as pages 137-138. Access by 🚗: following Car tour 4, leave Castelfranco di Sopra (the 112km-point) on the road to Pian di Scò and park 1km along, on the far side of the bridge. This walk follows quiet country roads and old mule tracks. From your parking place, follow the charming road signposted to Pulicciano (CAI 20) for 1h. Then continue uphill to where the CAI 33 track begins on the right. Follow the main walk from the just after the 3h30min-point to the 4h30min-point. At the road signposted to Caspri, descend to the right, to the main road. Then go right again, over the bridge, to your car.

This is a good walk when you really want to stretch your legs and get into your stride. It is one where you don't have to spend too much energy on finding the way — great if you want to think, or talk! It has two good climbs, but long stretches where the walking is easy, with the route laid out

TERRACES

Deep in the woods on a stony hillside, you will often see the remains of old terraces. It is not hard to imagine the intensity of the poverty and hunger that drove the people to such efforts to procure a little arable land. Today, their years of hard labour are disintegrating, as the rock walls fall back to the ground from whence they came.

The great terrace-building era was during the 17th and 18th centuries. Initially the peasants only piled up stones to make flat arable areas. But this later developed into some quite major engineering feats, as their skills developed.

Peasant families on hill or mountain farms would do some terracing each year. They began at the bottom of the hill, cutting out strips of soil and shoring up the lower edge with stone walls.

Typically the farmers used the terraces fully, planting a line of olive trees, a line of vines, and then wheat or other crop in the remaining space. Today only the olive trees remain, as their culture does not depend on tractors. Terracing not only gave more agricultural land, but helped to control soil erosion. It protected the soil behind the walls and slowed the rush of water after heavy rain. Now that the terraces are being neglected, we realise their value.

Photograph: terraced hillside above Castelfranco di Sopra (Car tour 4)

before your eyes. One of these is a ridge path across a long treeless moor, with magnificent and sharply-contrasting views. To the east are the higher mountains of the Pratomagno, sharp-edged and almost empty but for trees. To the west are the Chianti hills and the wide valley of the Arno, with its motorway, railway line, factories and people. And far into the distance, if it is a clear day, you can just see the tips of the Apennines, the Alpi Apuane and the sea. After all the exertion, the walk concludes easily, contouring along an ancient mule track which links the houses below the hill.

Start the main walk by the COMMUNAL RUBBISH BINS: follow the CAI 33 waymarkings up the road into the village, past characteristic stone houses. After veering to the right, you arrive just above the village of **Caspri**. Turn left here, leaving the upper part of the village on a road which soon becomes a dirt track. When

you come to a clearing in the pine woods, where there is a junction (**15min**), keep left and follow the track up to the road. Follow the road to the left uphill, to just past a house on the right with CAI WAYMARKS ON THE WALL (**25min**). *(Short walk 1 begins here.)* Turn right on a track just above the house and follow it around the fence of the property. Ignore the two tracks to the left. Notice the view of Arno Valley to the right now, where organ pipe-like cliffs of sand thrust up from the valley floor.

The track contours, crosses a stream and arrives at the hamlet of **Odina**, at a junction by a tiny CHAPEL (**35min**). Turn left up the track here for 5 minutes, until you are within sight of GREEN GATE-POSTS. Then take a grassy trail on the right (Picnic 11). This skirts the hillside until it arrives at a CONCRETE ROAD (**45min**). Walk round the barrier and follow the road to the left uphill. Ten minutes from the barrier, leave the road and turn right uphill on a steep shaly path. A couple of minutes later you with be within sight of a DERELICT COTTAGE.

The path continues behind the cottage at the edge of the escarpment and then runs up to the right, past some trees, to the SUMMIT of **Monte Cocollo** (874m/2866ft; **1h05min**). The summit ruins are a good place from which to enjoy the panorama towards the main ridge of the Pratomagno, its summit crowned with a cross.

Just beyond the first ruined wall, continue on the CAI 33, descending to the right. Two minutes later, when you meet a track (CAI 35; **1h10min**), follow it to the left, towards the ridge. You will follow this ridge track for 40 minutes, eventually climbing to the hill above (where you can see the obligatory masts). Ignore all other tracks until the track you have been following turns down to the right (**2h**). Continue straight ahead here, on a trail, keeping to the top of the ridge and following CAI waymarks on rocks and trees. Cross the saddle and scramble up the path to the road just below the summit of **Poggio Montrago** (1281m/4200ft; **2h45min**).

Now follow the road (CAI 20) to the left downhill for 45 minutes. Then turn left at a T-JUNCTION (**3h30min**). At the next junction, turn left again, on a cobbled mule track (CAI 33). *(Short walk 2 joins here, turning right on the CAI 33.)* This route contours along the side of the valley, crossing many streams, one of which has a pretty BRIDGE (**3h45min**) and a rock in a sunny spot, perfect for picnicking. From here continue past a CHAPEL to some cottages, where you turn left. Then turn left again on a road, into **Galligiano**. Pick up your contour-hugging track again on the right, opposite the CHAPEL in this hamlet. Ignore all other tracks going up or down the hill until you come to a Y-JUNCTION (**4h**): go right downhill here, past some gate posts, then cross another stream. At the next fork (**4h15min**) go right. After the track has rounded a pine-covered headland, you will arrive at your car below **Caspri** (**4h30min**).

This landscape of balze — great sandy cliffs eroded into spectacular shapes — lies on the southwest side of Castelnuovo di Sopra. The short walk on page 27 would take you there.

13 CIRCUIT FROM THE BADIA A PASSIGNANO

Distance/time: 14km/8.7mi; 3h35min (12km/7.5mi; 3h15min by car)

Grade: easy, with minimal ascents (200m/650ft overall). Almost all the walk is along easily-followed unsealed roads but, after heavy rain, you will have to slosh through huge puddles. Not suitable in high summer.

Equipment: as pages 137-138; also walking boots in wet weather

How to get there and return: SITA 🚌 349 from Florence to/from Sambuca; journey time 55min. Walk along Via F Rosselli, the main street which runs parallel with the Pesa. Follow the road upstream for 10 minutes, then join the main walk at the brick gatepost (the 2h30min-point). By 🚗: follow Car tour 2 *past* Panzano (78km) *and* the turning to Montefioralle, then turn left to Passignano. Park under the wall of the Badia.

Refreshments: restaurants/bars at the Badia and at Rignana

Note: The Badia a Passignano (see overleaf) is only open to the public on Sunday afternoons.

This is a walk full of variety; one that gives you a taste of some of the landscapes of the Chianti. You walk through shady oak forests, among smooth-sided hills lined with vineyards, over a flat flood-plain beside a swiftly-flowing stream, and up a rocky scrub-covered hillside. And that's not all; there is also a crenellated monastery at Passignano dominating the valley, a rustic trattoria with a veranda where you will want to linger and, most startling of all, a tabernacle in the middle of nowhere, with a serene fresco of the Madonna and Child by Neroccio di Bartolomeo.

Start the walk at the **Badia a Passignano**. Avoid, for the moment, the dual distractions of the Badia and the trattoria; walk uphill past both of them, to a Y-junction. Take the unsealed road to the right and follow it down into the valley and up the other side — a tough climb on a hot day. At the crossroads stay on the main unsealed road, veering left along STRADA RIGNANA (**30min**), following signs for the 'CANTINETTA RIGNANA'. At a second junction (**45min**), don't miss the frescoed TABERNACLE shown on page 89. Then turn right, still following the 'CANTINETTA' signs and the YELLOW ROUTE 4 TRIANGLES (a locally-waymarked route). You approach the *cantinetta* at **Rignana** (**50min**) via a road lined with an imposing wall and high cypresses. Beyond the restaurant, a panorama opens up, along the ridge towards Greve.

Take a minute to look at the portico of the little CHURCH just down the hill. The interior of the portico is elegantly decorated, as are the curved walls in front of it. As you ponder why anyone would put such an imposing entrance on a simple country church, continue along the unsealed road. Ignore all roads on either side. After passing the gates of the villa **Poggio alle Corti** (**1h15min**), still following the yellow triangles, veer right where the track starts to descend into fields and becomes much rougher underfoot. Then watch for a pillar on the right containing a mail box for the

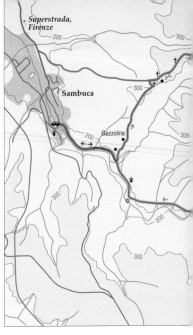

BADIA A PASSIGNANO

The Badia a Passignano is thought to be very old, probably eighth century, but written records only survive from medieval times, when it was sacked and burnt many times.

In the 10th century the monks accepted the strict reforms of San Giovanni Gualberto from Vallombrosa (who is buried in the Romanesque church). He demanded a war on the immoral behaviour of clergy and the scourge of simony — the selling of ecclesiastical privileges.

By the 1400s the abbey was well established, with its fair share of works of art, including a Last Supper by il Ghirlandaio. In 1810 Napoleon's policy of repression forced the monks to leave, and many great works were lost. The final indignity took place in 1870, when the whole place was sold at auction. A fake medieval tower was added in the 19th century, as was a castle-like facade. They do look rather wonderful, however, against the deep blue Tuscan sky.

Today the Badia is a parish of Fiesole and is run by a small community of Benedictine monks from Vallombrosa.

farm ahead (**1h20min**). Turn right here and follow the track down to the **River Pesa** (**1h25min**). Turn right along the right-hand bank of the river. Continue through the woods and keep left on the main trail in the floor of the valley — staying within earshot of the river. This part of the walk can be full of puddles, but you can often take a short detour round them.

Eventually a track comes underfoot. You skirt a renovated mill (**2h20min**), pass a CHAPEL, and cross a BRIDGE over a tributary. Turn right uphill on a trail beyond the bridge. You pass a brick GATE-POST (**2h30min**; *those who come by bus join here, turning left*) and a sign for 'GAZZOLINA'. Ignore the next trail on the right ... and the tempting swimming pool at the second house at **Gazzolina**, as you struggle up this once-cobbled trail. Near the top of the climb the way divides at a maze of bike paths. Follow the major path, keeping to the high ground. They all meet up

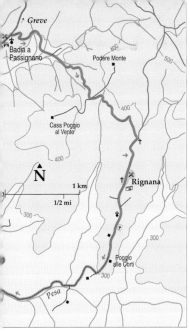

again where the woods finish and cultivated land begins (**2h55min**). In the distance you should see a farmhouse, with a tabernacle in the foreground. Follow the track to the left here, down to the road. Turn right towards the farm, set amongst glorious vineyard views, and walk back uphill to the **Badia** (**3h15min**).

Top: oratorio *near the end of the walk, with the Badia in the background.*
Bottom: tabernacle with fresco by Neroccio di Bartolomeo, near Rignana.

CHURCH BELLS

The tolling of church bells is very much a feature of life in Italy. Bells mark the passing of the day and the week.

For country people the bells were a vital means of getting information around the parish quickly. Codes of bell-ringing had special significance — the daily bells at noon called them home from the fields for a meal, while the Ave Maria marked the end of the working day.

Many of the church bells in and around Florence were made in England, long famous for its bell-making industry. Indeed some started life in the churches and monasteries in England but were sold off to Italians when King Henry VIII decided that England could manage with far fewer churches. New bells were also sold to Italy, sometimes as a means of exporting money which at that time was illegal. The Strozzi Family wanted to get some of their wealth back to Italy from England, so they imported bells which they immediately sold for cash in Florence.

14 CIRCUIT ROUND MUGNANA, LA PANCA AND SEZZATE

Distance/time: 11km/6.9mi; 3h20min

Grade: moderate, with an initial climb of 350m/1150ft. The walk mostly follows old tracks that link isolated farms and hamlets, and can be done in any season. Note that if you prefer a more gentle climb, do the walk in reverse, referring to the map: start in Mugnana, downhill from the castle. Drop down on a track into the olive grove near the sign pointing up to the church. Towards the end of the walk, don't miss the right turn, 10min past the Casa al Monte, that will bring you back to Mugnana.

Equipment: as page 137-138; also walking boots

How to get there and return: 🚗 only accessible by car: park at Mugnana (the 26km-point in Car tour 2), across the road from the castle, but further up the hill — just beyond the iron garage.

Refreshments: Trattoria Le Cernacchie at La Panca (good but fairly pricey); the bar at La Panca sells picnic food.

Longer walk: Mugnana — Rugliana — La Panca — Sezzate — Mugnana (14.5km/9mi; 4h40min). Grade, equipment, access as main walk. This extension of the main walk prolongs the time spent on the ridge but, as it is very wooded, there will only be views in winter. Just after Casa al Monte (45min), turn right at the T-junction, then turn left. Follow the main ridge track for 20min, then turn right downhill before the summit of Poggio di Rugliana. Turn left, round a house, in the tiny hamlet of Rugliana (1h45min). Descend this track to a sharp right-hand bend. Turn left here on the lower of two paths (the CAI 00; Picnic 6). Just before La Panca (2h05min), pick up the main walk at the 1h10min-point.

This walk is even possible in hot weather, if you make an early start. Most of the way is in shade, and the climb is at the beginning — while both you and the morning air are fresh. Path-finding is not too difficult, as the route circumnavigates the valley of the Sezzate River. The pleasures of this walk are typical of many walks in Tuscany. It evokes history — not so long ago in time, but aeons in civilisation. The trails followed link the isolated farms with each other and with the church and the mill. Though many of the houses are now beautifully converted, they have maintained their old-world atmosphere and character, clustered together into tiny knoll-top hamlets. Two fortress villas, a charcoal-makers' piazza, a ruined flour mill, and a water-bottling factory(!) complete the delights of the walk.

Start the walk on the road by the CASTLE at **Mugnana**: continue uphill along the road. Just before the gate of house number 188 on the left, your trail begins on the right (CAI 18; **5min**). You will follow this route for almost the entire walk (but note that the waymarks had not been refreshed at time of writing). The trail, cobbled in a pinky-purple stone, climbs and bends up the hill through the woods. Turn left at the first junction then ignore all the other paths leading off the main trail. Occasionally the climb relents, to give you time to catch your breath. At a T-JUNCTION, turn left (**35min**).

You are at the SUMMIT when you reach a derelict farm,

Casa al Monte, set back in cypresses (**45min**). It looks an idyllic place to live, when you are admiring the wonderful view, until you think about the practicalities — such as how one would get water here in the height of summer.

Almost within sight of the farm, the trail divides. Turn left to begin the gentle descent straight to La Panca (passing one of the settings for Picnic 6). *(But for the Longer walk, turn right here.)* On the outskirts of La Panca you meet a T-JUNCTION (**1h10min**), where the CAI 00 climbs up to the right. *(The Longer walk rejoins here.)* Turn left into **La Panca** and walk ahead to a crossroads. (If you want to stop at the bar, turn right here.)

To continue the main walk, keep straight on at the cross-roads, in front of the restaurant Le Cernacchie, on the road that climbs to La Sale. Watch for the CAI waymarks on lamp-posts. The asphalt soon runs out, and you enjoy a pleasant climb in the shade of oaks and pines, with a view down the Sezzate Valley to the left. Five minutes up the road you pass a WOODEN CROSS, by a track to the right. If you would like to see the church of San Pietro at Cintoia Alta, take a five-minute detour to the right here; otherwise continue to the left.

Watch out now for your ongoing trail which climbs to the left where the unsealed road bends to the right (**1h25min**).

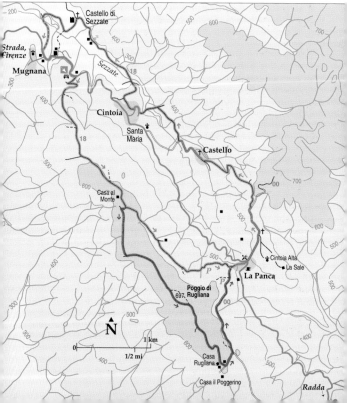

Strawberry tree, impressive drystone wall, and the bridge crossed en route to Sezzate

This stony trail soon starts to descend. Go left at the next junction (**1h30min**) and follow the trail into the charming hamlet of **Castello** (**1h30min**). Go through the hamlet, on past a large tabernacle, and down the track which continues straight ahead. Just before the track crosses a stream, turn right (YELLOW WAYMARK; **1h 40min**). Stay with this track as it contours along the right-hand side of the valley.

At a T-junction, turn left on the main track, cross the stream, and walk up into **Cintoia** (**2h**). The hamlet is not enhanced by the water-bottling factory, but it does have an 8th-century church and an elegant villa. Locate house number 44 in the piazza (on your right), and take the track at the side of it. Then turn left almost at once, then right on a track through a field. At the end of the field (from where there is a lovely view of the Chianti), you come to a T-JUNCTION: turn right here, back down towards the river. (But look back, too, to admire the beautiful villa.)

After the track bends to the left, there is a junction with a track coming up from the river (**2h15min**). Follow this downhill for a couple of metres, then fork left on an initially unpromising path. Follow this to the left of a huge V-shaped rock ... and suddenly you will come upon a cobbled mule track bordered by a wall which would dignify an important thoroughfare. This is the trail to Sezzate. It crosses the river via the graceful bridge shown above, with water cascading down over huge rocks (after rain). At the clearing by a pool further down the trail (**2h30min**), take time to look around. There are the ruins of a tiny mill at the right of the trail, the perfect place to take a rest. Across a wooden bridge there's a bonfire piazza and a replica of the temporary dwelling a charcoal-maker (see page 71) would have built while working here.

Further along the shady mule track there is a house with a water trough (the icy water is very cooling on a hot day). Then **Sezzate** rises before you, with its monumental fortified residence (**2h50min**). Walk up to the barrier across the road to the castle, then turn left down a trail through olive groves. This track veers right towards the castle wall, then drops into the valley. Cross the stream at the ford, then follow the main trail up through fields, circling round the back of the wooded hill crowned by Mugnana's castle. When you meet the road in **Mugnana** (**3h20min**), turn left uphill to your car.

Above: olive skin residue after pressing

OLIVES AND OLIVE OIL

These soft silvery-leaved trees have been an essential part of Tuscan life since ancient times. They flourish in a Mediterranean climate. Thankfully for Tuscany they are very shallow-rooted trees, so they survive on rocky soils. Generally they tolerate frosts and snow, although in 1985 a particularly vicious frost in the Florence area killed 17 million of the 22 million trees. It was devastating for the farmers, but when the dead trunks were cut down, new shoots appeared and these grew into some of the trees we see today.

The younger trees tend to be kept small in size for easier harvesting. The gnarled specimens, full of character, are some of the ancient trees that survived the 1985 frost and others.

Olives ripen in the late autumn, when their colour begins to change from green to black. The longer the fruit is on the tree, the higher the oil content, varying from 12 to 20%. The first fruits are picked green.

The oil from these olives has a more pungent flavour than those harvested black. Indeed locals assure me that oils from different areas have very different flavours. The method of harvesting also affects the flavour. The 'crème de la crème' is the oil from hand-picked olives, which have never fallen to the ground and been bruised. The method most used in Tuscany produces the next-best oil: the fruit is 'combed' off the branches, letting the olives fall into huge nets (or old parachutes!) encircling the trees. The fruit can also be encouraged to drop by 'caning' the tree ... or it can just fall into the net.

It is important that the fruit is processed as quickly as possible, and certainly within 10 days at most. Nowadays the machines that smash the oil from the olives are powered by electricity rather than animal- or water-power. The traditional method was 'cold-pressing' — squeezing the olives between heavy grinding stones vertically rotating inside a huge bowl. The resulting mush was spread onto round rope mats that were loaded into the press. A huge screw was then turned to force out the oil. Today the oil is usually extracted by centrifuge and hydraulics. The first pressing, *extra vergine,* is the best oil. It is dark green and cloudy when new, with a peppery flavour that can be quite a shock to strangers, but is much appreciated by the locals. They hold parties to celebrate the new oil, eating it soaked into slightly garlicky toasted bread, called *fettunta.* As the pressing continues, the oil has less colour and flavour and becomes more acidic. *Extra vergine* has an acidity of less than 1%, *vergine* less than 2%. All other grades of olive oil are made from high-acid oil in which the acidity is chemically corrected and deodorised.

Olive oil does lose its flavour over time. It lasts about 18 months if it is stored in a cool dark place. But who can keep it that long?

15 CIRCUIT FROM GAIOLE VIA THE CASTELLO DI MELETO AND BARBISCHIO

Distance/time: 12km/7.5mi; 3h15min

Grade: easy, with an ascent of 200m/650ft; on good tracks and trails and suitable in any season

Equipment: as pages 137-138; also walking boots if there has been rain, as there is a ford to cross

How to get there: TRA-IN 🚐 127 from Siena to/from Gaiole *(not Sundays);* journey time 50min. Or 🚗: following Car tour 2, turn off to Gaiole at the 53km-point; park on the road behind the church.

Refreshments: bar/restaurants in Gaiole; pizzerias at Barbischio and Castagnoli (the latter called L'Alto Chianti)

Note: Meleto Castle can be visited on a guided tour (groups only); tel: 0577 749217 to enquire about the fee and opening times.

This walk is set in the heart of Chianti and the Chianti Classico wine-growing area. The route has all the ingredients for a typical Chianti walk. It starts in a stone-paved piazza, passes a 10th-century church, a castle involved in the wars between Siena and Florence, and a medieval tower house. It is, of course, set among a myriad of vineyards patterning the hillsides not covered with trees. In autumn, with all the wild fruits around — blackberries, figs and grapes — the walk is a feast both metaphorically and literally.

Start the walk in the centre of **Gaiole**, by the SCULPTURE. This street, VIA CASABLANCA, is the main road to Siena (SS408). Follow this road towards Siena until you arrive at a JUNCTION (**5min**). Stay on the right-hand side of the road, cross VIA GALILEI, and look straight ahead for your ongoing route — a track that starts at this junction and winds uphill. It passes a renovated FARMHOUSE and leads into the piazza of the 10th-century parish church of **Spaltenna** (**15min**). The surrounding buildings are now a hotel, so are very well kept. Take the track at the right of the piazza, skirting the HOTEL COMPLEX, with the hotel grounds and gardens on the left and a vineyard on the right. Veer to the left at the POND and continue to where the main track turns left: go straight ahead here on an old grassy track into the trees, leaving the CAI 16 behind. Soon you join a second track, where YELLOW MARKERS indicate the line of an underground pipe. Emerging from the trees, you will see a large derelict FARM on your left. Head towards it, skirting the edge of VINEYARDS (**25min**).

The farm is **San Pierone** and, if it is still uninhabited, do look around the outside. You will see the outdoor oven, the wells, and a chapel. It looks as if the people left only recently. Head left downhill from the farm, towards a strange, isolated villa with a tabernacle at the crossroads.

(The last time we did this walk, land was being cleared for new vineyards, and the stone tabernacle had been moved — temporarily I hope!) Continue with the villa's garden wall on your left, the *cantina* for 'Geografico' wine on your right, and the castle of Meleto on the hillside ahead. What could be more Chianti? The track leads you into the valley, skirting to the right of a FARMHOUSE halfway down (**40min**).

Meeting the Siena road once more, go left and immediately right over the bridge (signposted for Meleto). Five minutes up this minor road, you pass a derelict building on the right: it was the lime kiln for plaster for the walls inside Meleto castle (photograph below). Plans are now afoot for it to be turned into a restaurant. Turn right up the straight, cypress-lined drive leading into the courtyard of the **Castello di Meleto** (**55min**).

After a tour (see above) and perhaps a wine-tasting, follow the CAI 56 along the chapel wall. This track has wonderful views over the undulating Chianti country with its woodlands and vineyards. The track leads past a farm and

Top: old lime kiln for plaster for the walls inside Meleto Castle; bottom: looking towards the castle across typical Chianti vineyards

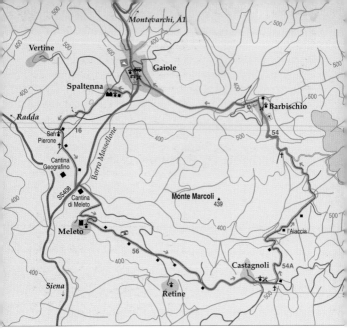

up to another, large rectangular farm on the ridge. The track dips and then rises to the road again, by a BUS STOP (**1h15min**). Cross the road and follow a track towards another farm. The track divides below the farm: keep left and continue, veering right, back to the road. Turn left on the road and stroll up to **Castagnoli** (**1h45min**), with its huge castle-like building by the roadside. Below the wall you can see some of the stainless steel wine-making equipment.

Walk straight on, past the church and restaurant. Just before the next house on the left (where there is a WOODEN CROSS on the opposite side of the road; **1h50min**), turn left down a track, the CAI 54A. Cross the stream by the ford, then walk up to a pretty HOLIDAY HOME (**2h05min**). Beyond the next house, the track becomes a sandy trail through chestnut woods and scrub. Follow this marked route, ignoring two trails off to the right, until you meet a wide track. Turn left here; then, at a wide junction with a TABERNACLE (**2h35min**), take the right-hand track (CAI 54).

Coming into the medieval hamlet of **Barbischio**, you meet a Y-junction (**2h45min**). The road to the right goes up to the 10th-century tower house; take the road to the left, descending past the Papavero Restaurant. The road ends by 'PIETRO', a house covered with old farming artefacts. But a lovely soft woodland trail continues to the right and takes you down to the stream. Turn left, walk parallel with the stream, and you will come to a farmyard, which was once the old village MILL (**3h**). Continue down to the road and turn right over the bridge. At the T-JUNCTION, keep left for **Gaiole** (**3h15min**).

VINEYARDS

Virgil said 'Vines love an open hill', so what better place to grow grape vines than in Tuscany.

Grape vines, which naturally are woodland climbers from lowland areas of the Mediterranean, have many other requirements if good grapes are to be harvested.

These include: a great deal of light, a warm climate (between 25 and 28°C in the growing season), abundant autumn sunshine to ripen the fruit, well-drained soil to encourage the roots to grow deep into the subsoil, plenty of water, and moving humid air. Of course the plants love rich soil in which they produce strong verdant growth. Wine-growers, however, would rather they produce grapes, so prefer less-rich soils. It is no wonder that much of Tuscany produces good wine, with its rolling hills, dry gritty, sandy soils, proximity to the sea with its warm breezes, and protection by the Apennines from the worst winter weather. But late frosts, hail storms and unreliable spells of rain occur too, just to stop the growers from getting too complacent.

The wild strain of grape, *Vitis vinifera,* is indigenous to Italy and parts of Asia, and still grows wild here. Italians were not in fact the first wine-makers, but have certainly been developing their skills for thousands of years. Production of wine today is not dissimilar to the methods used by the peasants over centuries. Winter and spring is the time for pruning and training the vines. Today concrete posts and wire hold up many new vines, but you can still see plants trained onto specially-pollarded turkey oak trees using willow fronds — the time-honoured method. Spring is spraying time, and autumn is harvest time (the *vendemmia*). In Tuscany, this is still done largely by hand by groups of grape-pickers, although I have seen one huge machine. Recently the quality of Italian wine has improved drastically, due to new methods of viticulture and oenoculture. Large estates now exist where the only crop is grapes. They produce homogeneous, dependable wines at a reasonable price. Extremely high quality wines are also produced in estates where the wine-makers have experimented with using different varieties of grape, adding Cabernet Sauvignon grapes for example, to the traditional red Sangiovese. Making good-quality wines on well-run vineyards is one of the few agricultural enterprises in Tuscany that can actually make a profit.

16 CIRCUIT FROM MONTE SAN MICHELE VIA VOLPAIA

Distance/time: 13km/8mi; 3h25min

Grade: quite easy, with an ascent of 280m/920ft. Half of the walk is in shade and half in sun: if you are walking in summer, use the map to do the walk from Volpaia, so that you can climb in shade.

Equipment: as pages 137-138; also walking boots after wet weather

How to get there and return: 🚗 only accessible by car: park at the car park below the summit of Monte San Michele (the 48km-point on Car tour 2). If you are doing the walk from Volpaia, park there: at the 58km-point in Car tour 2, follow signposting first for Greve, then Volpaia.

Refreshments: at San Michele, Baddiaccia and Volpaia

Longer walk: Monte San Michele — Volpaia — Radda — Monte San Michele (27km/16.7mi; 7h). Grade as main walk, but very long, with an overall ascent of 500m/1650ft. Equipment and access as main walk. When you reach Volpaia, pick up Walk 17 at the 2h05min-point, follow it back to Volpaia, and then continue this walk.

We first did this walk on a perfect autumn day, when cumulus clouds filled the sky with movement and beauty. Initially the route descends a long-forgotten but once important mule track, winding down and round the upper Pesa Valley — past deserted houses, across streams, and through shady woods. From the tiny photogenic hamlet of Volpaia, you climb back to the summits, surrounded by hilltops bright with heathers, rose hips and leaves turning colour. Beyond are long views of blue hills, sheathed in woods and punctuated by stone villages.

Start the walk at the CAR PARK below **Monte San Michele**, where the CAI 00 and CAI 9 both cross the road. Walk down the road and turn right into the little *borgo* of **Badiaccia** (**5min**), once a Camaldose abbey. Just past the *osteria*/bar, descend steps to the road below and turn right. This road soon becomes a gravelled track; it was once the main cobbled road to Volpaia. After it bends to the left, it begins its descent towards the valley. After passing through a wood-yard, turn right at a junction with another gravel track (**20min**). When you reach an isolated house, walk between the barn and the house, then turn left below the house. After crossing a stream, the trail arrives at the ruins of **Dògole** (**30min**), with its tiny-roomed houses filled with ivy. Walk to the right of the houses and below a high wall, then veer right, to cross another stream. The now-cobbled mule track swings left, deep in the woods, and ascends to a ridge and a JUNCTION (**40min**), where you fork left. Just before the trail swings to the right through overhanging broom, ignore a path to the left (**45min**). Your trail curves down into the valley, before crossing a series of tumbling streams (**55min**).

Soon after joining a track coming from the left, you arrive at **Casa Lusignano** (**1h 20min**), a very well-kept house with

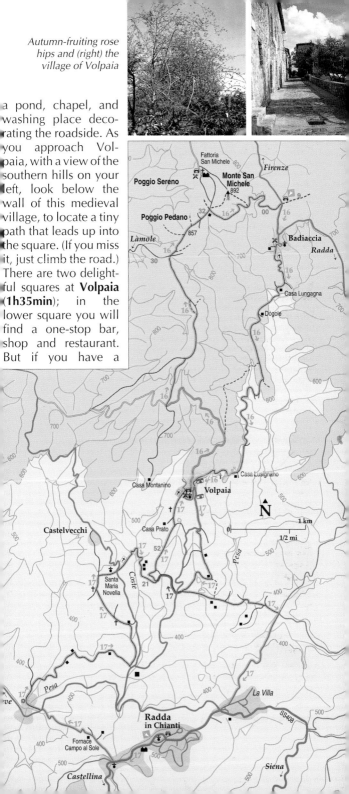

Autumn-fruiting rose hips and (right) the village of Volpaia

a pond, chapel, and washing place decorating the roadside. As you approach Volpaia, with a view of the southern hills on your left, look below the wall of this medieval village, to locate a tiny path that leads up into the square. (If you miss it, just climb the road.) There are two delightful squares at **Volpaia (1h35min)**; in the lower square you will find a one-stop bar, shop and restaurant. But if you have a

IRIS *(Iris germanica variation florintina)* As its Latin name suggests, this flower is very significant for the people of Florence. It has been the symbol of the city, used on flags and the coat-of-arms since medieval times.

Its distinctive shape and colour are perfect for use in heraldry.

Iris grow prolifically in this area, decorating the edges of lanes and paths, but this variety was cultivated for its essential oil — not only used in perfumes and soap, but added to poorer-quality wines to give them 'nose'. You can still find it growing wild today, flowering from April to June, filling olive groves waist-high with its purple flowers.

The hoopoe bird *(Upupa epops)* is a fairly common summer visitor to Tuscany. It reminds me rather of a 15th-century courtier, with its long haughty beak and its smart cockade of feathers. Its breast and body are cinnamon in colour, but its wings are bold black and white stripes, stripes that are echoed on its crest and tail. This 'designer bird' arrives in the late spring to live around farmland and to nest in holes. Its long bill is used to extract insects and larvae from soft earth. Obviously its name comes from its cry, which is a 'hoo-hoo' sound.

picnic, sit on the sunny bench just below the 'CASTELLO VOLPAIA' sign. The castle was involved in the frequent battles between the Guelfs and Ghibellines and was plundered many times.

To complete the circuit, head uphill, away from Volpaia's church tower, on the road called VIA DEI POGGI. It soon becomes a quiet, unsealed road, with open views all around. Follow it for about 2km, to a bend where the community RUBBISH BIN stands (**2h10min**). Ignore the trail on the left just beyond the bin (signposted to 'MONTANINO', but take the wide rocky trail on the right here, climbing uphill through Mediterranean scrub. When you come to a track, turn right: this wide, waymarked (CAI 32), high-level track leads all the way back to San Michele and is well-used by outdoor people of all passions.

Ignore a track to the right (**2h 34min**) and other forest trails. When you join a track coming from the left (from Làmole; **2h 48min**), continue on the higher of the two tracks ahead. You are now gently climbing pine-capped **Poggio Pedano**. The track enters the trees, then veers to the left of the summit. It dips to a muddy clearing, then rises again to a second open area with a WOODEN SHELTER (**3h**) and a major junction. Ignore both a path and the first track to the left; the second track to the left leads to San Michele's hotel and amenities. The path straight ahead climbs to the radio masts (where there is no view). Take the CAI 00 track to the right: it leads back down to the CAR PARK (**3h25min**).

17 CIRCUIT FROM RADDA VIA VOLPAIA

See map page 99

Distance/time: 14km/ 8.7mi; 3h30min

Grade: Easy, typical undulating Chianti walking, with overall ascents of 400m/1300ft, along old mule and cart tracks. Not suitable in mid-summer, as there would be too much climbing in full sun.

Equipment: as pages 137-138; also walking boots after rain, as you have to wade across a river

How to get there and return: TRA-IN 🚌 125 from Siena to/from Radda *(not Sundays)*; journey 1h. Or 🚗: park outside the village walls at Radda (the 55km-point in Car tour 2)

Refreshments: 'La Bottega' in the lower square at Volpaia (shop, bar and restaurant)

Short walk: Volpaia — Santa Maria Novella — Volpaia (5.5km/3.5mi; 1h 45min). Easy; equipment as pages 137-138. Access by 🚗: park at Volpaia (see page 98). Follow the main walk from the 2h05min-to the 2h30min-point, then turn right to the road. Cross the road and follow a good track to the church of Santa Maria Novella. To return, follow the main walk from the 1h20min-to the 2h05min-point, partially retracing your route.

Longer walk: Radda — Volpaia — Monte San Michele — Radda (28km/ 17.3mi; 7h). See Longer walk 16, page 98. From Volpaia, join Walk 16 at the 1h35min-point.

Cypresses at Settignano (Walk 2)

CYPRESS TREE *(Cupressus sempervirens)*
Surprisingly, this tree which seems to symbolise Tuscany, is not a native. It is thought to have been introduced into Italy from Asia Minor by the Etruscans. Since then it has held an important place in the practical and spiritual life of the people of Tuscany.

The Romans planted cypresses around the tombs of important people. Perhaps this is the origin of their other name, 'cemetery pine'. In ancient mythology they also symbolised life, as they are evergreen, long-living, shaped like a flame, and their wood is very resistant. Traditionally they have been planted to celebrate the birth of a child and to mark a sacred or important place.

The practical uses of the tree were not wasted on the Tuscans. Its distinctive form and the great height to which it can grow (50m/165ft) make it the perfect tree for a landmark, defining the end of a property, a road, or an important shrine.

The cypress has been very useful for reforestation, as it can survive on thin compacted soils and tolerate long periods of cold. Today, however, the future of the cypress in Tuscany is uncertain, as the trees are being devastated by two maladies. A fungus, *Seiridium cardinale,* spread by burrowing insects, is causing the trees to rot and to 'bleed' their resin. Agricultural experts tried planting a resistant variety of cypress, only to find that it is particularly susceptible to *Cinara cupressi,* an aphid which sucks the sap and turns the tree a rusty colour. Many of Tuscany's cypresses are dying. Even if the experts find a remedy soon, the landscape is bound to suffer in the short term. Cypresses are expensive to buy, need a long time to grow, and prefer clean air.

This walk takes you from one medieval hilltop village to another, and for much of the hike you can see your route laid out before you — first Volpaia lying lazily on the massive bulk of the Chianti hills below Monte San Michele and, on the homeward trek, Radda, rising along a ridge on the horizon. The route is full of varied landscapes and terrain, but always in 'classic' Chianti wine-growing land.

Start the walk in **Radda**, leaving from the front of the town hall (PALAZZO DEL PODESTA) in the VILLAGE SQUARE. Walk west out of the village, heading downhill on VIA ROMA. At the first junction, continue straight ahead past the RELAIS VIGNALE HOTEL on the left, to the next major intersection, where there is a tiny CHAPEL. Take the road opposite the chapel, signposted 'FORNACE (pottery) CAMPO AL SOLE' (**10min**), dropping down to the right. Passing the pottery, you reach the road to Greve.

Cross the road and then take the gravel track slightly to the left. Follow this across the Pesa River, to a OLD MILL (where barking dogs will announce your approach). The track goes between some buildings, then rises to the left of the mill house with its pond (**25min**). The track now begins to climb more steeply, but leave it after three minutes: take a rough trail on the right, heading down to the left of a pasture. Stay with this trail as it crosses a stream and climbs past two farmhouses (the first with a wonderful clutter of old farm machinery). Pass to the left of a THIRD FARM (**50min**) and continue towards the road.

Just before reaching the road, take a track on the left. It climbs through oak woods to the edge of a vineyard, then heads towards an imposing villa. Pass below the high villa wall (**1h**) on your right and continue uphill towards an oak

wood. The track divides here. Go left into the next vineyard, but stay alongside the wall on the right and continue to climb, to a junction with a pink and blue TABERNACLE (**1h15min**). Fork right here and, further on, turn right through gates and walk downhill through fields, to the 12th-century church of **Santa Maria Novella (1h20min)**.

Round the church and cross the road. Then take the soft grassy trail opposite, dropping gently into the Coste Valley.

Vineyards in the sun, on the final stretch along the road back to Radda

The trail widens out and crosses two bridges over tributaries, then rises. Ignore all side-trails until you come to a T-JUNCTION (**1h40min**) with an important track. Signposting on a rock here indicates 'SANTA MARIA NOVELLA' (the way you came) and 'VOLPAIA'. Turn left uphill towards Volpaia, and go left again after 200m/yds, passing signs for various old farms (now holiday homes), all part of the Volpaia estate. Follow this track (CAI 52), keeping left at another junction, all the way to **Volpaia** (**2h05min**). You come into the village on VIALE DEL NONNO (Grandfather's Street), which leads to the cemetery — a memorable lane lined with stone walls and complete with an arch.

When you are ready to head back to Radda, take the road to the left of the restaurant in the piazza. Walking down this road, surrounded by a horseshoe of hills and the rich texture of woods and vineyards, is a delight. At a sharp bend in the road (**2h10min**), you will see two tracks on the left. Take the second track (the one nearest to the road, with a sign 'STRADA PRIVATA' to discourage motorists). Follow it downhill past a hut. Go straight ahead at a junction, heading down through vineyards. The track skirts a well-maintained house on three sides, then continues to a T-JUNCTION (**2h30min**).Turn left here. *(But go right for the Short walk.)* Pass a small reservoir and come to a farm (now a HOLIDAY CENTRE; **2h40min**).

Walk between the buildings and straight down to the Pesa River. Cross the river, then follow the track in a curve to the left, through a plantation. Turn right at a junction, then rise a little before descending to a ROAD (**3h**). Turn right: from here it's a gentle climb of just under 3km/2mi along the road (keep straight on at all junctions) back to **Radda** (**3h30min**).

18 CIRCUIT FROM SAN DONATO (NEAR SAN GIMIGNANO)

Distance/time: 8.5km/5.3mi; 2h

Grade: easy, along farm tracks, with an ascent of only 100m/330ft; a good walk for all the family and suitable all year round.

Equipment: as pages 137-138

How to get there and return: 🚐 only accessible by car. From San Gimignano (the 21km-point on Car tour 5), take the road to Volterra. Park just beyond San Donato, where the lower road from the village joins the main road; there is space by the communal rubbish bins.

Refreshments: *osteria* at San Donato (but opening hours are erratic)

Longer walk: San Gimignano — Montauto — San Donato — San Gimignano (15.5km/9.7mi; 4h). Grade and equipment as main walk; access by TRA-IN 🚌 from Siena to/from San Gimignano or 🚐 (as above). Walk along the road signposted to Volterra for 1km, then go left towards Montauto. At Montauto turn right. Follow the main walk from the 45min-point to the end, then retrace your steps to San Gimignano.

This most pleasant of walks combines perfectly with half a day's sight-seeing in San Gimignano. The route is a circuit made up of two stretches along hilltops joined by a quintessential Tuscan lane that crosses the Bagni Valley. It is all set amidst vineyards and wide fields of cereals, with the landscape right up to the Apennines laid out before you.

Start the walk in the hamlet of **San Donato**. Walk past the tiny CHAPEL hemmed in by a house, then descend the second

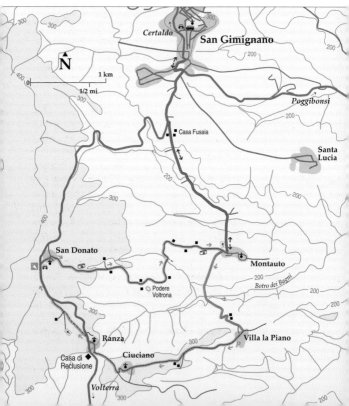

COUNTRY DWELLINGS

Exploring outside the towns, you may notice that the old dwellings you see out in the countryside seem to be of four distinct types — relics of the crop-sharing system, *mezzadria* (page 57). The largest and most imposing dwelling was the villa, the home of the landowner. Situated nearby was the *fattoria*, often the largest farm. The hub of the estate, it housed the wine and olive presses, granary, wood store and carpenter's shop. Here the *fattora*, or estate manager, lived with his family, as did other salaried employees such as the game-keeper. Smaller farms were the homes and work places of the peasants who crop-shared with the landlord. These farms are the *casa colonicas* which convert so beautifully into holiday homes. As many as 16 people may have lived there, with the cattle stabled on the ground floor. The kitchen, the warmest room, was the centre of the home. Benches were often set into the walls by the fire, with the only other furniture being a big table, a sink and a bread-kneading trough. The kitchen was on the first floor, together with many two-bedded rooms, the granary, a room to lay out olives, and a *loggia* or

Well over cistern at Rocca d'Orcia (Walk 23, Car tour 7)

covered terrace where work could continue during bad weather. Farmhouses were very basic, draughty, cold in winter and dirty. Cleaning was not a priority, as water and time were scarce. Everywhere would have been blackened by smoke from the all-important fire. Outside was a stone terrace, used as a threshing floor and surrounded by out-buildings, barns and stores. It was vital that there was a water source nearby, a stream, a well or a cistern for water collected from the roof. The bread oven was usually outside, set into the house wall.

The fourth type of dwelling you might see are workers' cottages, the homes of farm labourers not a part of the family at the farm. Often these tiniest of cottages were not as comfortable as the cattle stalls tucked warmly under the farm kitchen.

track to the right, signposted 'FATTORIA VOLTRONA'. This breathtaking track starts by a well, where hens run about freely. It continues with views of San Gimignano, evoking medieval times, when armies marched these hills with drums rolling. It ends after passing several farmhouses beyond the farmyard of **Podere Voltrona** (**27min**). Here the only option is to continue downhill, veering left along the side of a fence (CAI-waymarked). Cross the stream bed and head left uphill on a track between rows of vines. Follow the track to the right, to a house, and then towards the church of Montauto sitting comfortably on the knoll ahead.

Within sight of the ROAD TO MONTAUTO, turn right downhill on an unsealed road (**45min**; *the Longer walk joins here*). (Or first keep ahead to visit the church at Montauto.) Follow this quintessential Tuscan lane, lined with cypresses of course, across the Bagni stream and up the far side of the valley, to the **Villa la Piano** (**1h05min**). Here take the track

BURRAIA
This small building was the country folks' 'fridge', used to keep food cool in the summer. Designs vary, but essentially it was storage space often set in the hillside with stream water running through. As the water ran through a series of stone sinks with wooden shelves above, it evaporated and lowered the air temperature, keeping it under 6-7°C in summer — as long as the stream didn't dry up! If there wasn't a convenient stream, food was kept cool by storing it down the well or above the cistern. Today you can still find *burraia* — often along mountain tracks — struggling to hold themselves together.

on the right, signposted 'CIUCIANO'. As you start along this wooded level track (Picnic 12), you pass a CROSS set in a base of bricks. Ignore all turnings left and right until you come to a Y-junction by an ARTIFICIAL POOL (**1h20min**). Keep right here.

The track reaches the hamlet of **Ciuciano** (**1h30min**), where your arrival will be greeted by a cacophony of barking (but the dogs should all be fenced in). This is a fascinating ancient hamlet, as authentic as any you will find in Tuscany. As you wander down the hill, you will notice an incongruous modern complex across the road. It is a *casa di reclusione,* a prison. What a pity the wonderful views can't be enjoyed by the residents.

Turn right at a T-junction, then leave the main track as you approach the road: take the rough track ahead, into and through the hamlet of **Ranza** (**1h40min**). At the end of this village, follow the road to the right uphill. But when you come to the top of a tiny triangular vineyard, cross the road and take a track up to the left — an ancient cobbled trail that passes through a wild rock-garden. All too soon you meet a proper track. Follow it to the right and, when you come to the road, turn left to **San Donato** (**2h**).

Looking across the Botro dei Bagni, below Montauto

19 CIRCUIT FROM THE WALLS OF VOLTERRA

Distance/time: 11km/7mi; 3h15min

Grade: quite easy, with an ascent of of 350m/1150ft. Suitable all year round. This walk is described with the climb at the end, but you can also begin at the bar/restaurant 'Prato d'Era' (just north of Volterra on the S439d), in order to do the climbing first, enjoy a little sight-seeing in the middle, and then finish with a relaxing descent.

Equipment: as pages 137-138

How to get there and return: TRA-IN 🚌 from Colle Val d'Elsa or SITA 🚌 from Florence to/from Volterra. Or 🚗: park at Volterra (the 53km-point in Car tour 5), at one of the car parks outside the walls.

Refreshments: bar/restaurants in Volterra; bar/restaurant at Prato d'Era

This pretty walk starts at one of the gates to Volterra and will combine easily with half a day's sightseeing in the town. The route descends along a winding paved track which serves only a few houses set deep in countryside. You glide easily downhill, looking out towards far-off hills blanketed with fields of cereal crops. A dark volcano-like mountain dominates the horizon. At the halfway point in the walk you can stop for a coffee. Then you begin the wonderful climb from the river back to Volterra, on a cobbled mule track — the Via Salaiola, supposedly of Roman origin. From a tumbling stream, the route passes Etruscan tombs and takes you through the Etruscan Diana Gate and into the city by the medieval gate.

Start the walk at **Volterra**, at the 'PORTA A SELCI' GATE below the MEDICI FORTRESS. Walk through the gate, then down a flight of steps on the left. Turn left on the main road, towards Siena. Carry on down past the Esso petrol station, to the corner of VIA L SCABIA (signposted to the church of SAN GIRO-LAMO; **10min**). Turn left on this road (red and white CAI waymarks), winding down into the valley through ilex woods and old olive groves, between sandy cliffs. As it is a cul-de-sac for vehicles, this is a very quiet road.

Beyond a CHURCH with an impressive portico, you pass a large empty HOSPITAL complex and, later, its neglected ceme-tery. Towards the bottom of the hill, watch out for the old stone *lavanderia* (washing place) on the right (**1h**) — a huge rectangular sink with sloping scrubbing-stones at the edges, all sheltered by an awning of vines. Around the bend, just below a house, turn sharp left on a track. Follow the red and white waymarks: they lead you round and below a second house, where you ignore a grassy track to the left. At a Y-JUNCTION, head left downhill to the main road (S439d; **1h10min**).

Turn left and follow the road along the flat Era Valley to another road junction, where you turn left to the bar/restau-rant 'PRATO D'ERA' (**1h30min**). From here take the track on the left, just above the restaurant's boundary hedge. Soon

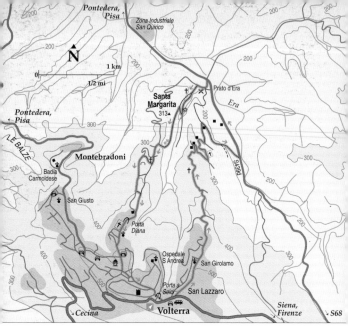

you will see the ancient mule track back to Volterra, on your right. But I suggest that you join this mule track a little further on, since the walk beside the stream is so pleasant: continue on the main track, past several houses, until you come to a beautifully-preserved old MILL. Follow the stream briefly, to your ascending trail — it is on your right and marked by CYPRESS TREES (**1h40min**). As you round the first sharp bend, the old mule track you spotted earlier comes up from below to join you. The route is now clear; always keep uphill, on the old cobbles. Just past a DRINKING TROUGH with a stone crest, the track turns to the right, up to a road (**2h**).

Follow this road for three minutes but, just before a TABERNACLE, turn off left, to join a second mule track climbing the hill (ignore a fork to the left where this track bends to the right). Join the road again and turn left, passing two sign-posted Etruscan cave-tombs on the left (they are illuminated, but unsupervised). As you continue up the road, watch for more caves in the embankment. Leave the road some 600m/yds along, at the second track to the left. When you meet another road, turn right uphill towards Volterra.

You walk through the Etruscan gate, the PORTA DIANA (**2h 55min**). Go on past the flower-filled cemetery and follow the steep old RAMPA DELLA COCINA past a CHAPEL. In no time at all you are back at the medieval city wall and the PORTA FIORENTINA at the entrance to **Volterra** (**3h15min**), with the ruins of the Roman amphitheatre to the right. Walk up to VIA MINZONI and follow it left to the PORTA A SELCI. Go through the gate and down the steps, to the CAR PARK AND BUS STOP.

The ancient mule track to Volterra

The ruined Badia Camoldese above the balze, *the eroded cliffs near Volterra (Car tour 5)*

UMBRELLA OR STONE PINE *(Pinus pinea)*

There can be no doubt which pine this is, with its distinctive shape, so poignant when growing alone, yet so neighbourly when in a group, the shape of one mirrored in the next. They are not native to Italy but have been grown here since Roman times.

These trees are the source of the pine nut or *pinoli*. Harvesting the nuts was an arduous task in the past. It took place between the grape harvest and the olive harvest. The entire family was involved: fit young men climbed the tree to knock down the cones with a stick. The family took them home and heated them in the fire to persuade them to open and give up their precious seeds. But the seeds, covered in soot and pine resin, were still enclosed in a hard case that the peasants had to crack open. Often they ground the kernels into flour or used them whole, much as we do today. These pines were of no other use to the country people, as the wood is too hard and heavy to work.

20 CIRCUIT FROM MONTE OLIVETO VIA SAN GIOVANNI D'ASSO

Distance/time: 17km/10.5mi; 4h45min

Grade: fairly easy, with an overall ascent of 320m/1050ft. Except for the first section, all on good tracks and unsealed roads. The initial descent, on a steep and indistinct path, can be avoided by walking along the road to Chiusure. Suitable all year round, except in high summer

Equipment: as pages 137-138

How to get there and return: 🚌 from Siena to/from San Giovanni *(only on weekends from May to October):* telephone the Siena tourist office for details: 0577 241254; start the walk at the 2h20min-point *(and see also Short walks 1 and 2 below).* Otherwise by 🚗: park at Monte Oliveto, the 35km-point on Car tour 6.

Refreshments: restaurant at Monte Oliveto Maggiore; bar (with a good view and groceries for sale) at Chiusure

Short walks

1 San Giovanni — Monterongriffoli — San Giovanni (5km/3mi; 1h30min). Easy, with an ascent of 80m/260ft; Equipment and access as main walk; park in front of the castle at San Giovanni (the 43km-point on Car tour 6). Follow the main walk from the 2h20min-point to the 3h-point, then turn left. Keep to the main track until you meet an unsealed road. Turn right to explore Monterongriffoli, an unspoiled agricultural hamlet now almost unpopulated. Return on the same unsealed road all the way to the main road, then turn left back to San Giovanni.

2 San Giovanni — San Marcellino — San Giovanni (7km/4mi; 2h). Easy, with an ascent of 120m/400ft; equipment and access as Short walk 1 above. Follow the main walk from the 2h20min-point to the 3h40min-point. At this three-way junction, turn right and pick up the main walk again at the 1h40min-point, to return to to San Giovanni.

3 Monte Oliveto — Chiusure — Monte Oliveto (5km/3mi; 1h30min). Moderate, with an initial descent on a steep, faint path and an ascent of 200m/650ft. Follow the main walk to Chiusure (1h). To return either follow the road (see walk at the 4h20min-point), or retrace your steps.

T his dumbbell-shaped walk gives you the opportunity to explore the Sienese Crete in depth. Travelling from a 14th-century monastery, the route descends to the base of a ravine where groves of poplar trees are protected for the precious crop of white truffles harbouring beneath them. The route climbs to a tiny fortress village, then crosses a plateau of huge fields split by deep ravines. Some ravines are wooded, but others are bare beige-to-grey clay — remin-

Monte Oliveto Maggiore

The Sienese Crete, bare clay ravines

iscent of the 'badlands' in cowboy films. It is a high-level walk, where the land, dominated by the extinct volcano of Monte Amiata, is laid out before you like a map.

Start the walk in the car park at **Monte Oliveto Maggiore**: cross the drawbridge of the gatehouse decorated with a lovely Della Robbia statue of Mother and Child. The stone and brick road leads down to the church, past an information office and a shop selling products made by the monks. After visiting the CHURCH, take the gravel track heading off at 90° from the building (signposted to the Monks' Cemetery). A third of the way along, you pass a picnic table on the left, made from a stone grinding-wheel.

Your indistinct path to Chiusure begins here. Turn half-left (45°) downhill through trees, heading below the end of the monastery. You cross a flat terrace, heading in the direction of the monastery. On the right is an overgrown track. Turn left along this track, towards a large brick out-building with CAI way-marks (the last building in the monastery complex; **15min**). Take the track running alongside the

Monte Oliveto Maggiore, although set among dense trees, has dominated the landscape in this part of Tuscany since the early 14th century.

In 1313 a group of devout merchants from Siena, led by Giovanni Tolomei, decided to establish an order of Benedictines on this site. Building of the monastery went on throughout the 14th century, until this grand brick edifice rose in all its aloof dignity.

The church was completed by 1417 and is now famed for the exquisite wood inlaid choir stalls by Fra Giovanni da Verona. More famous perhaps are the frescoes that decorate the walls of the Great Cloister. Some were painted by Luca Signorelli, the first nine scenes depicting the life of St Benedict. More colourful are the remaining 27, painted by Il Sodoma, full of very elegant young men and wonderful landscapes. (Find among them the artist's self-portrait, in white gloves and with his pet badger!)

Today the few monks that remain restore books and sell their honey and wines in their shop.

The monastery is open to the public every day from 9.15 to 12.00; a Gregorian chant is sung at 18.00h in summer and 17.00h in winter.

'Private truffling' sign (RACOLTA DI TARTUFI RISERVATA) *by the stream below Chiusure*

TRUFFLES

From September to December, under cover of darkness, men set out with dogs to hunt one of the most valuable food-stuffs in the world. They are not seeking wild animals but the Tuscan white truffle, *Tuber magnatum pico*.

This exotic beast is a round knobbly fungus that grows underground, attached to tree roots. When the fungus is mature, it produces a characteristic odour that attracts animals. They eat the truffles and spread the spores. Luckily the hunters can train their dogs to seek, find, but not *eat* the truffles.

As truffles are spoilt by heating ... and cost around 1000 dollars a pound, they are used raw and very sparingly.

If you can afford some, slice it paper thin onto ready-cooked dishes such as pasta, risotto or eggs. The main areas where truffles are found in Tuscany are San Giovanni d'Asso, south of Siena and San Miniato near Pisa.

Truffles are also thought to be a powerful aphrodisiac!

bottom of this building, heading downhill. At the first junction, take the lower track to the right. Follow this main track to a Y-JUNCTION: go left here through high sandy embankments. This pretty track, lined with tall grasses and trees, winds its way down to a stream with a dam. Cross the STREAM (**30min**) either above or below the dam. Then turn left and begin the climb, veering to the right, with the small valley on your left. The CAI markings stop for a while here. The climb ends on the ridge (Picnic 14), where you turn left on an unsealed road.

When you meet the road at **Chiusure** (**1h**), turn right into this charming brick-built village, passing a well and coming to the piazza (where there is a bar with a fine view). Continue ahead until you are within sight of the 'STOP' sign, then turn right on another unsealed road (in front of houses 46 and 48).

From here on the route undulates gently along the tops of plateaus, with vast panoramas in every direction. Still within sight of Chiusure, take a track on the left (this junction is marked by a 'PROVINCA DI SIENA' NOTICE BOARD with two confusing maps; **1h20min**). Keep right at the next junction two minutes along. Continue round the bend, to see San Giovanni in the distance. Turn left at a junction with WOODEN HANDRAILS. Beyond the crest of the hill, you come to a THREE-WAY JUNCTION (**1h40min**). Descend the middle, broom-lined track and, at a fork, turn right through a WOODEN GATE. Stay on this track until you are directly below the village of San Giovanni, then turn right at a T-JUNCTION. This track takes you to the base of the huge CASTLE below **San Giovanni** (**2h20min**). *(Short walks 1 and 2 begin here.)* To

look at the village go left, otherwise turn right downhill to the main road, then turn right again along the straight road signposted to Siena.

Once you have crossed the stream, take the first right turn, an unsealed road climbing to **Ferrano** with its villa (**2h 50min**). Beyond the villa and its outbuildings, the track divides. Keep right and, when you reach a track on the left coming from Monterongriffoli (**3h**), keep right again. *(But Short walk 1 turns left here.)* The main track leads past some farms and to a tiny chapel on the left, **San Marcellino (3h 15min)**, surrounded by a mass of cypresses. Just beyond it, turn right on a track. Some 500m/yds along, ignore the track to a house on the right; cross a hill and return to the three-way junction encountered earlier (**3h40min**). *(Short walk 2 turns right here, using the notes from the 1h40min-point.)* Retrace your route from here to **Chiusure** (**4h20min**). Then either keep retracing your steps (the track to the monastery is on the left), or continue along the road, turning left at the junction overlooked by the 'dark praying lady', back to **Monte Oliveto Maggiore** (**4h45min**).

21 FROM MONTALCINO TO THE ABBEY OF SANT'ANTIMO

Distance/time: 9km/5.6mi; 2h30min

Grade: easy, through gently undulating countryside along very well signposted tracks and trails. Total ascent of 140m/460ft. One stretch of very eroded track makes it unsuitable for those who are not steady on their feet. Suitable all year round.

Equipment: as pages 137-138

How to get there: TRA-IN 🚌 from Siena to Montalcino; journey time 1h20min. Or 🚗: park at the castle at Montalcino (the 9km-point on Car tour 7), first making sure that the return bus is running (see below).
To return: TRA-IN 🚌 from Sant'Antimo to Montalcino *(Mon-Fri only, at 14.25 and 16.50; recheck times);* collect your car there, or change buses for Siena

Refreshments: restaurant 'Osteria Basso Mondo' at Castelnuovo

Short walk: Sant'Antimo — Castelnuovo — Sant'Antimo (2.3km/1.4mi; 35min. Easy stroll. Access: 🚗 to Sant'Antimo (the 18km-point on Car tour 7). Follow the short walk described on page 34; perhaps combine it with nearby Picnic 16 (notes page 11).

The abbey of Sant'Antimo is one of the most beautiful churches I have ever seen. Not only is it set perfectly in a bowl of gently curving fields, but its interior has simple strong lines rising, it seems, to Heaven. Other decoration is only simply-carved capitals, rounded window arches and the natural stone, all of which seem to mirror the simplicity of the landscape outside. To arrive there on foot makes your approach all the more fitting: you can imagine yourselves pilgrims, as you round the hillside to see the church below, perhaps framed by hillsides sparkling yellow in their autumn colours and with Monte Amiata as a backdrop. If you visit on a weekend when there is no bus, it is no hardship to walk back, as the terrain is varied and the views wonderful. Approaching the walled hilltop town of Montalcino at dusk, you can anticipate a glass of the famous Brunello di Montalcino — after all, you will have earned it!

Start the walk in **Montalcino**. Facing the castle at the top of the town, take the narrow road at the right of the castle wall, going under an arch. When you come to a lower road, turn left, to a road junction. Now follow the road signposted to 'GROSSETO' for one minute, then turn right on VIA DEL POGGIOLO, which is well waymarked by the CAI. (The Province of Siena also waymarks this route, but the maps on their notice boards seem to confuse more than clarify.) Walk past the CEMETERY and on to an unsealed road. Cross straight over the first junction, heading up to a house on a knoll. When you reach the house (CASA DUE PORTE), keep right at a fork. Follow this track until you are stopped by a CHAIN BARRIER (**15min**) marking the boundary of the house ahead and the start of the avenue of cypresses. Your ongoing path, on the left, skirts the property. It is badly eroded above a

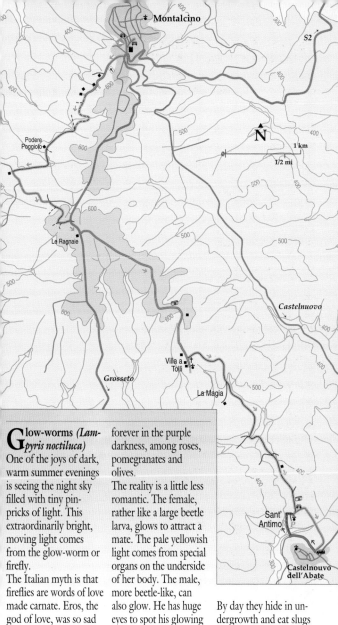

Montalcino

N

0 | 1 km

1/2 mi

S2

Podere
Poggiolo

La Ragnaie

Castelnuovo

Villa a
Tolli

Grosseto

La Magia

Sant'
Antimo

Castelnouvo
dell'Abate

Glow-worms *(Lam-pyris noctiluca)*
One of the joys of dark, warm summer evenings is seeing the night sky filled with tiny pin-pricks of light. This extraordinarily bright, moving light comes from the glow-worm or firefly.

The Italian myth is that fireflies are words of love made carnate. Eros, the god of love, was so sad that fireflies died, he deemed they should live forever in the purple darkness, among roses, pomegranates and olives.

The reality is a little less romantic. The female, rather like a large beetle larva, glows to attract a mate. The pale yellowish light comes from special organs on the underside of her body. The male, more beetle-like, can also glow. He has huge eyes to spot his glowing love and can fly, unlike the female.

By day they hide in undergrowth and eat slugs and snails (and puppy dog tails).

horse paddock, but soon arrives at an old mule track through ilex woods. Keep left at all junctions, until you arrive at a fenced-off farm (**30min**). Continue down to the road and turn left (**40min**).

There is now a spell of road walking, straight uphill, ignoring a road on the right. Cut a bend off the road by taking a track to the right. This short-cut is signalled by a Siena 'ROUTE 2' sign (**50min**). Go straight over the first junction, then turn left on a gravel track that leads left, back down to a road. Turn right and follow the road uphill for another five minutes, to an *agriturismo* — 'LE RAGNAIE' (**1h**), a farm on the right which provides holiday accommodation. Take the unsealed road to the left here, wandering gently along the hilltops. Relax and enjoy the long views towards Pienza and the Apennines on the left, and the old volcano of Monte Amiata ahead. The track arrives at a traditional farm, with geese, hens and lots of dogs wandering about. Pass a junction with a WOODEN CROSS and walk on into **Villa a Tolli** (**1h30min**), a cluster of houses and a tiny church.

Return to the wooden cross and turn right at the junction: this track descends to another *agriturismo,* 'LA MAGIA' (**1h 50min**). Fork left before the building, dropping more steeply now. This very eroded section needs a little extra care, especially if you would rather enjoy the view. Go left at the following junctions, always keeping to the left of the stream, until you arrive at the church of **Sant'Antimo** (**2h20min**; Picnic 16).

Once you have immersed yourself in the beauty of the place, continue to Castelnuovo, the hilltop village you can see above. There *is* a path, but take the road you can see dividing the fields: it gives the best views. The BUS SHELTER is

at the road junction just below the entrance to **Castelnuovo del'Abate** (**2h 30min**), and the restaurant is to the left.

To walk back to Montalcino, return to Sant'Antimo the way you came or use the map to follow the road and then a path beside the stream. From Sant' Antimo just follow the waymarks, but don't miss your right turn up to the eroded track (25min) just before the stream crossing. At the end of the middle stretch of road, your right turn is signposted to Poggiolo (1h50min) and, in the woods, don't miss your right fork, just before before a rivulet (2h05min).

Winter: vineyards beside Via del Poggiolo in Montalcino (top left), and eroded path above the horse paddock (right). Autumn: vineyards near Sant'Antimo (middle), and the abbey church (bottom)

22 CIRCUIT ROUND BAGNO VIGNONI

Distance/time: 10km/6.2mi; 2h35min

Grade: fairly easy, with one ascent of 200m/650ft. Suitable all year round, except for high summer

Equipment: as page 137-138; also optional bathing things

How to get there and return: TRA-IN 🚌 from Siena to/from San Quirico d'Orcia; journey time 1h25min, then RAMA 🚌 to/from Abbadia San Salvatore; alight at Bagno Vignoni; journey time 10min. (Also one direct bus a day: leaves Siena at 10.45 and returns at 18.05; *recheck locally!*) Or 🚗: park at Bagno Vignoni (the 105km-point in Car tour 7)

Refreshments: bars and restaurants in Bagno Vignoni. The 'Bodega di Caccio', between the old and new baths, provides good picnic food to eat in or take away.

Short walk: Bagno Vignoni — Orcia River — Bagno Vignoni (5km/3mi; 1h20min). Easy, with a short ascent of 80m/260ft; equipment and access as main walk. Follow the main walk to the river crossing, and return the same way. Children should love this short walk, where they can explore a derelict factory, broken suspension bridge, and old mill; there are also places to swim or paddle.

Longer walk: Figure-of-eight from Bagno Vignoni (22km/13.7mi; 6h05min). Moderate-strenuous, with an overall ascent of 540m/1770ft. Equipment and access as main walk. If the river is low, cross at the ford (the 37min-point) and do Walk 23; then complete this circuit.

This is an opportunity to combine a well-signposted walk through varied landscapes with much of historic interest with a bathe in mineral water heated by the remains of a volcano. Be sure to look at the old baths, but swim in the new one (in the Hotel Posta Marcucci and open to non-residents). This outdoor pool allows you luxuriate in steamy water while enjoying the landscape, dominated by a distinctive castle. If you prefer to bathe more informally and for free, just pop in the little pool below the hill at the start of the walk.

Start the walk in **Bagno Vignoni**, above and in front of the HOTEL POSTA MARCUCCI. The warm water flows in a conduit along the street here, then slides over limestone rocks into the valley. To get to the track below, walk downhill on

Bagno Vignoni

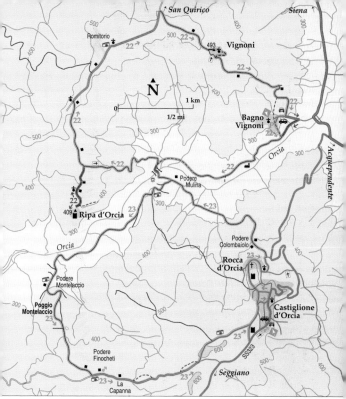

the steep path on the left-hand side of this overflow. You will pass the pool shown overleaf, where you can bathe, perhaps after ending the walk. (If you find this path too steep, walk down the road towards the main road.) Whether you take the path or the road, turn right on the first track you meet. Follow this track, keeping parallel with the river (unfortunately not *beside* the river, although you will have the sound of flowing water all around you).

After passing a sad, DERELICT FACTORY (**25min**), keep right on the main trail, heading up and over rocks, into the woods. Follow a path along the edge of a field, watching for red and white CAI waymarks. Beyond more fields and woods, the muddy trail comes to a T-JUNCTION (**37min**) within sight of the SUSPENSION BRIDGE shown overleaf. Your ongoing route is to the right, but first *do* explore to the *left,* where a track crosses the River d'Orcia via a concrete ford. *(The Longer walk crosses here, to pick up Walk 23.)* These shallows, difficult to cross after heavy rain, were once the site of a very important river crossing, as you can see from the forlorn ruins of the suspension bridge (still usable if you are James Bond) and the supports of an old stone road bridge washed away in a flood. An abandoned mill is just across the water. *(The Short walk returns now to Bagno Vignoni.)*

Top: view through reeds to Rocca d'Orcia (Longer walk); middle: the pool at the start of the walk; bottom: the suspension bridge near the ford, with Rocca's castle in the background

From here walk back to the junction and continue up the stony track, only used these days by hunters with four-wheel drive vehicles. When you reach a cypress-lined derelict CEMETERY (**1h10min**), with old headstones lying around, you are almost at the top of this prolonged climb. At the nearby junction, the main walk turns right. (If you have time for a 30-minute return detour, first go *left* on the unsealed road to the castle of Ripa d'Orcia, now a hotel. It once controlled access to the strategically-important Orcia Valley, and its spectacular view down the gorge is worth the deviation. The path to the viewpoint is to the left of the main castle entrance, but take care, it is a very steep drop.)

Turning right at the junction, follow the track gently uphill past *agriturismo* farms. At the highest point in the walk, you come to a tiny CHAPEL (**1h25min**) with a ring of cypresses behind it and views of Montalcino ahead, backed by the strange landscape of the Sienese Crete. Keep right on the unsealed road from the chapel, to a JUNCTION (**2h10min**), where San Quirico is ahead and Vignoni to the right. Head right into **Vignoni**, a medieval hamlet with a fortified tower, a few houses and a church. Walk through the hamlet, under the gate by the church, and then down the path to the right; this brings you back to the main track, by the cemetery. Continue left downhill to **Bagno Vignoni (2h35min)**.

120

RELIGIOUS STREET FURNITURE

Some of the most attractive and intriguing street furniture in Tuscany, especially to anyone not from a Catholic country, are the religious edifices — the shrines, tabernacles, and tiny chapels that exist along the wayside. So much religious faith, so much devotion, so much invention and energy to build them all. Deep spirituality and religious faith were central to the lives of the peasants. The Church built the parish churches, but the peasants used their own energy and expertise to build what they needed to be able to make their faith an active part of their everyday life. Of course the landowners were also responsible for religious buildings, often family chapels.

Shrines were often built close to barns and stables, and dedicated to helpful saints such as San Vincenzo Ferrer, protector of the harvest, or San Antonio Abate, protector of animals.

Niches containing perhaps colourful glazed plaques dedicated to the Virgin Mary decorated the farm wall. Here the women especially could show their devotion, by keeping the niche supplied with fresh flowers and candles. The Virgin Mary was then ever present around the home to be called on for help and protection in times of trouble and to be thanked for all their blessings.

Free-standing **tabernacles** often marked a place of some significance, either religious (the site of a miracle or of a special religious festival), or terrestrial (at, for instance, a water source or a crossroads). The earlier tabernacles would have contained frescoes, many of which have now disappeared either into dust or been stolen. Important frescoes have been transferred to art galleries for safe-keeping. Glazed porcelain images and terracotta pictures replaced them, especially in areas close to pottery towns such as Impru-

neta. Where frescoes remain, they are either copies or behind glass although, amazingly, one can still come across a beautifully frescoed 14th-century tabernacle, some still open to the elements (see page 89). When the tabernacle was the gift of a wealthy family, the fresco was often encased in elegantly-carved marble or stone, and would have included the coat-of-arms of the family.

In places of greater spiritual importance, local artisans built small **chapels** or oratorios (see page 89), often very simple in design, with only an altar and a space for the worshippers. Their charm emanates from the simplicity of the design and the faith they represent.

The resouceful people of the Apuane mountains had the good sense to combine a shelter with a shrine. These *marginette* provide both physical and spiritual protection along once-important mule tracks, as on Walk 7.

23 CIRCUIT OF THREE CASTLES, FROM CASTIGLIONE D'ORCIA

See map page 119; see also photographs pages 34-35, 105, 120

Distance/time: 12km/7.5mi; 3h30min

Grade: easy-moderate, with an ascent of 340m/1115ft. The walk follows mule tracks deep in the woods for much of the time, and is suitable even in high summer. See also Longer walk 2 below.

Equipment: as pages 137-138; also sunhat for the last stretch (in full sun)

How to get there and return: TRA-IN 🚌 from Siena to/from San Quirico d'Orcia; journey time 1h25min, then RAMA 🚌 to/from Castiglione d'Orcia; journey time 12min. Or 🚗 to/from Castiglione (the 102km-point on Car tour 7); park on Viale Marconi, on the southern edge of the town, just by the information office, which is also Bar Petra.

Refreshments: bar/restaurants in Castiglione and Rocca

Longer walks

1 **Figure-of-eight from Bagno Vignoni:** See Longer walk 22, page 118.

2 **Bagno Vignoni — Walk 23 — Bagno Vignoni** (17km/10.6mi; 4h 30min). Grade and equipment as main walk. Access as Walk 22, page 118. Start out early at Bagno Vignoni (see Walk 22), cross the river via the ford, and pick up this walk at the 1h10min-point. This allows you to get the climbing over in the cooler part of the day. Return to Bagno Vignoni when you get back to the ford.

Note: the castle at Rocca (small charge; photograph overleaf) is open to the public every day, 10.00-13.00 and 15.00-19.30.

Dominated by three fortresses, this walk has a true medieval atmosphere. You wander through the ancient streets of the castle-topped villages of Castiglione d'Orcia and Rocca d'Orcia, the latter built high on a rock of solid limestone and dominating the landscape (photograph page 120). An old road, now only a track, takes you down to a once-important river crossing littered with the remains of defunct bridges. Along the mule track, deep in the woods, the silence of the route evokes times gone by, when travel was lonely and adventurous. A third castle, at Ripa d'Orcia, keeps watchful eye on your progress: it seems so close that you could reach out and touch it, although it is on the far side of a gorge.

Summer landscape below the castle at Castiglione d'Orcia

Start the walk at the CAR PARK in **Castiglione d'Orcia**: turn right along the main road (SS323) towards Siena, with the old village up to your left. At the ERG petrol and *carabinieri* stations turn left on VIA DELLA ROCCA, then go right in front of the bakery (where they make a wonderful whole-wheat bread, *pane integrale*). At the crossroads, continue straight ahead, curving round to the left and below the great fortress at **Rocca d'Orcia**. Drop down left into the medieval hamlet; its piazza is dominated by a well, still filled with dark water (photograph page 105). Leave the hamlet by following BORGO MAESTRO to the right, going down through an arch to a CHAPEL at the corner of a street (**25min**). Turn left here and follow the road until you come to a well-signposted track on the left, with a walkers' notice board. Follow this track, which links the Colombaiolo and Mulina farms and ends at a ford at the **Orcia River** (**1h10min**), near the suspension bridge shown on page 120.

If the water is low, it is easy to cross the river paddling over the concrete ford, to link up with Walk 22. *(Both Longer walks cross here, from Bagno Vignoni.)* In the trees on the left, beside the river, there is a derelict mill buried deep in the undergrowth. Take a peek, but don't go inside: the beams are not to be trusted.

Now return to PODERE MULINA (the last farm you passed), and take the track heading off to the right (marked with the red and white flashes of the Amiata/Senese route). The route undulates, more or less parallel with the river, although not in sight of it. It is a wonderfully quiet woodland trail. At time of writing it was very well waymarked but, just in case the marks fade by the time you use this book, note the following junctions where *care is needed,* especially as the trail can be overgrown in summer. Fifteen minutes from the ford (**1h25min**), the main trail leads right; continue up to the *left* here, then turn right at a T-JUNCTION, up through the

'ILEX TREE';
HOLM OAK
(Quercus ilex)
When reading descriptions of the Tuscan landscape, the 'ilex tree' is often mentioned, as it is so commonplace in the landscape. The tree is indigenous, growing wild in wood- and scrublands below 600 metres. They are in fact, evergreen oaks so look rather sombre except in the springtime. Then the shiny new light-green leaves contrast pleasantly with the dark green of the old leaves. Its acorns are tiny and pointed. The tree likes warm dry weather and fortunately it can tolerate city pollution.

Town hall in Castiglione d'Orcia (left) and view from the castle at Rocca d'Orcia

Willows are one of the joys of winter walking, when their golden-red young branches shine boldly against the muted shades of an otherwise dormant landscape. Willow trees are regularly pollarded to produce supple new shoots, for ease of working. The thin branches are used as twine, to train vines along their supports, as well as for making baskets and fencing. The white willow (*Salix alba*) is the one you will mostly see growing at the edge of fields and along streams, almost always pollarded into a gnarled stump topped with a mass of straight young branches sprouting from the top. Willows have another important use: their roots consolidate the ground in which they grow, thus helping to prevent soil erosion in times of flooding.

woods. The track arrives at a KNOLL (**1h30min**) with a far-reaching view — a good picnic spot. Ignore the track continuing uphill; instead, take the right-hand track and turn right again at the next FORK (**1h40min**) — all the time avoiding climbing the hillside to the left.

There are two streams to cross, although you may not notice them in summer. After the second stream, take the small path to the right for a minute, to the river bank, where you can admire the gorge and the water. Then return to the main track, to begin the climb. Fairly soon (**2h05min**) you will meet an important track on a bend: follow it to the left uphill and keep left at the next fork. The climb ends momentarily at a derelict farm, **Podere Montelaccio** (**2h20min**), with a spectacular all-round view. Pass between the house and an out-building with a perfectly-domed bread oven. The track divides here: go left, curving uphill. Ignore the first left turn towards a field. At a Y-JUNCTION (**2h30min**), choose either way: the sunny track to the left or the shaded trail to the right. Both routes climb a short way, rejoin, then descend to a POND. You will see the route ahead, absolutely straight, at the side of a pine wood. When you come to a big RED BARN (**2h50min**), you are almost at the top of your climb. The unsealed road is just up ahead, and a glorious view greets you there: Monte Amiata is to the south, surrounded by a vast sea of hills.

To return to Castiglione, turn left on the road — quiet, but very hot in summer. At a major junction, both forks lead

124

TRACKS

Many of the tracks and trails followed on these walks originated when farms were built and needed linking to neighbouring farms, fields, the *fattoria* (see page 57), the church, and the village. These trails often run straight past the main door of the farmhouse. In fertile areas, the land became divided into ever-smaller units, each with its own roads, so in some areas a network of tiny, tortuous roads exists. All roads to the church were designated 'community roads', so are protected against closure.

Paved roads and even narrow mule paths were uncommon, except along major trade routes or roads to important religious and secular centres. The paved country roads lined with strong stone walls are probably medieval. Indeed there is an hypothesis that in medieval times parishes, the units of civil organisation, were deliberately planned to include a major obstacle to transport such as a river or a mountain. It is thought that this encouraged the people themselves to build roads and bridges to join the parts of the parish together, thus improving the infrastructure of the whole area.

Podere Colombaiolo, the farm below Rocca d'Orcia

As in Roman times, each village or parish was responsible for a stretch of road. Inevitably, medieval roads followed many of the ancient routes already established by the Etruscans and the Romans before them. The Via Cassia, through Bagno a Ripoli, is one such route.

Vie di transumanza, transhumance routes along which cattle were seasonally herded, are now quite important trekking tracks. Sheep were moved each autumn and spring from the mountains to the coastal salt marshes of the Maremma along these tracks. One such road goes through Bagno a Ripoli to Grassina and on to the Chianti at the Passo di Pecorai (Shepherds' Pass).

As time passed, the importance of roads changed with patterns of use. Once-important routes — like the old cobbled roads with stone drinking troughs by the wayside, deep in the middle forests — are now neglected, as are the mountain tracks made by the charcoal-burners and chestnut-gatherers. It is sad to see these old tracks, built over so many years of hard toil, being abandoned by all but hikers.

to Castiglione, but the left-hand road is quieter. Take this, but rest a while to enjoy the landscape, with Montalcino towards the left and Ripa's castle-hotel and Bagno Vignoni to the right. The route ahead to Castiglione and its castle is obvious. Keep to the left until you see the arched stone gate into **Castiglione (3h20min)**. Go through the arch, descend to the right through the old square, and follow BORGO V EMANUELE to the PARKING, BUS STOP and BAR.

24 CIRCUIT FROM VIVO D'ORCIA ON THE SLOPES OF MONTE AMIATA

Distance/time: 14.5km/9mi; 4h30min

Grade: moderate, with an ascent of 350m/1150ft. Suitable all year round, except in snow and on the hottest summer days

Equipment: as pages 137-138; also walking boots

How to get there and return: RAMA, TRA-IN or 'Bargagli' 🚌 from Siena to/from Buonconvento, then 🚌 to/from Vivo d'Orcia (*weekdays only*; enquire in advance at the tourist office in Abbadia San Salvatore; journey time about 1h45min). Or by 🚗: park in the car park just below Vivo d'Orcia, on the road from the SS2 (the 71km-point in Car tour 7).

Refreshments: none en route; water available at the forestry refuge

Short walk: Vivo d'Orcia — Ermicciolo — Vico d'Orcia (4.5km/3mi; 1h30min). Easy, with an ascent of 130m/425ft. Equipment as pages 137-138; access as main walk. Follow the main walk to the 25min-point, then go left to pass the spring (Picnic 17) and a sign, 'Vivo 1.5km'. Five minutes later, when the track begins to descend straight ahead, take a track to the right (*not* waymarked). When you reach a stone forest hut, veer left; continue (now waymarked) to the road and back down to Vivo.

When the southern plains of Tuscany are too hot and crowded, this is just the walk to revive your spirits. It is a triangular route on the slopes of the extinct Amiata volcano, which is a ski resort in winter. The entire route is above 800m/2600ft and largely in the shade of feathery beech tree leaves. Although they cast plenty of shade, they still afford a feeling of light and space, as their canopy is so high and the trunks so tall and straight. This is not a strenuous walk, but one full of peace, quiet and interest. Dry stream beds come underfoot (many of the streams are now piped to provide water for Siena); cliffs and huge rocks are scattered like pebbles on the mountain slope. When you leave the tree cover for the open heathland, views of receding blue hills await you. One of the highlights in the landscape is the stubby rock on which the town of Radicofani rises.

Start the walk in the CENTRE of **Vivo d'Orcia**: go left towards Abbadia San Salvatore at the crossroads, then right to the CHURCH. Take the road opposite the church (red and white CAI/Provincia di Siena waymarks). The road soon becomes a grassy track. Five minutes along, descend a rough path to the right. (If it is too rough for you, take the next path on the right.) You come to an attractive dell, a cool spot in summer. Cross a dam, then climb steps and a slope, up to a stone terrace. A waterfall is up to the left, with picnic tables set among woodland paths (Picnic 17). Take the track leading away from the waterfall, walking along the terrace until you meet a wide gravel track. Go left uphill here, past rocky cliffs, to the road. Turn left on the road and left again almost immediately, on a track signposted 'SORGENTI (springs) DI VIVO'.

At a FORK (**25min**), keep right uphill, through gate posts. (*The Short walk keeps left here, and the main walk returns*

126

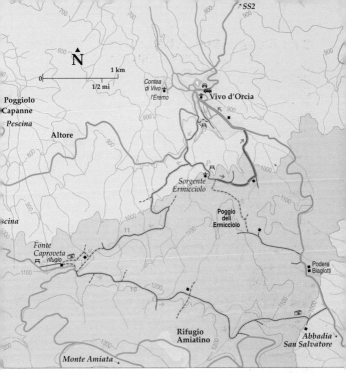

this way.) You now begin a steady climb on a clear forestry track sheltered by beech trees. Follow the red and white CAI 11 WAYMARKS, ignoring all tracks on either side. The route keeps to the right of high cliffs. Some 50 minutes uphill, leave the track: turn left on a well-waymarked PATH (**1h15min**), heading towards a low crest. As the path begins to climb a steeper slope (by a dry stream bed), turn right downhill on a second path (also waymarked; **1h25min**). Follows the dry valley to a WATERWORKS BUILDING, then turn left on a contouring trail. It soon becomes a grassy path with good views towards Castiglione.

A charming stone forestry refuge, 'CAPROVETRA' marks one corner of the walk's triangle (**1h35min**). If you need to replenish your water bottle, there is a tap ahead, by the road. Turn left along the far side of the refuge, climbing a path parallel with the road. When you join the road, on a sharp bend, take another CAI trail off left into the forest, to continue climbing to the left. This area is full of forest tracks, so keep *carefully* following the red and white waymarks (now CAI 10) on this undulating trail, winding your way in a generally easterly direction. At time of writing there was only one place where the markings were not clear: at a Y-JUNCTION (**2h 15min**), many *orange* markings indicate a right turn. *Do not* turn right here; go left, and you will soon see the red and white CAI waymarks again. As you arrive within ear-shot of

Top left: rocks and beech trees on the slopes of Monte Amiata. Picnic 17: bridge over the dam (top right), chapel of Ermicciolo, near the Sorgenti di Vivo (above right) and (left) the waterfall by the first set of picnic tables, 10 minutes from Vivo.

the road, take a trail down to the left through a stand of tall pines (still CAI 10; **2h35min**). (If you reach the road you've gone too far.) This trail marks the second corner of the triangle.

As you descend, with the dry valley on your left, stop a moment at a wide flat area, with a low stone wall and a few seats (**2h45min**). Here the route turns down sharp left, to cross a little valley and rise up the other side, alongside an old wooden fence. The marked trail comes out of the woods to an open heath and welcome views. Take the trail straight down to a track, turn left, and walk to the road (**3h05min**).

Follow the road to the left — a steep climb, and in full sun. After 10 minutes, beyond a roadside farm, take the *second* track to the left (Provinca di Siena notice board and waymarks). Walk through trees to a JUNCTION (**3h30min**), where both forks are waymarked. Turn right here (beside a fence), then *carefully* follow the red and white CAI waymarks through the woods. When you meet a T-JUNCTION (**3h55min**) signposted right to 'VIVO D'ORCIA' and left to a spring, chapel and picnic area, go *left*. Visit the **Ermicciolo chapel** if you have energy for the short climb, then follow the track back down to the fork first encountered at the 25min-point and retrace your steps to **Vivo** (**4h30min**).

Peasant life was a life of never-ending toil, the monotony broken only by events in the farming calendar or religious festivities.

Babies were born, sons preferably, then kept away from the dangers of light and air in their covered cots. Children joined the work force as soon as possible, tending animals and collecting firewood or wild food. Schooling, if any, was rudimentary.

Young people had a chance to look each other over at the dances that were a part of many festivals. Courting, however, only took place after church on Sunday or when there was a *festa*. There was not much choice of future partner. As country people rarely left their immediate environment, they could look only within their own parish or the next. Often they had no choice at all; the father made the decision.

One old peasant, who lives just 20 minutes by car from Florence, told me that she didn't visit the city until she was 42. When it was her time to find a partner, she had no choice. Both her parents died when she was 14. Her family then had to leave their farm, so she moved to the next farm and married their son.

Fiancées met on Sundays, when the boys had lunch with their future in-laws. The girl did not see her new home until after the wedding. Her work continued much as before, except that she was now answerable to her mother-in-law. Little wonder young couples left home as soon as possible after World War II.

Women did the most work, as they had to labour in the fields as well as care for the home and family. When the day's work was over, they could relax … with a little basket-weaving or sewing. There was little time, energy or water for such luxuries as cleaning the house or washing.

Life for all the family was focused on the farm and the church. Only the head of the family, dressed in his best, went to market. Peddlers played an important role in country life. The housewife could buy much of what she needed from one of these travelling salesmen, using what little money she had earned from the sale of eggs or honey. Services such as knife-sharpening, music-making, fortune-telling, and the weaving of chair-backs were all supplied by itinerants. Religion, superstition, magic, and medicine seem to have been interlinked for country people. The local witch-doctor/herbalist was generally the first port of call when someone was sick. Forests as well as foreigners were treated with suspicion. Forests were the home of untamed nature, full of hostility and evil, the home of witches and snakes.

Such isolation inevitably affected the character of the peasant people (*contadini*), who have been variously described as 'illiterate, stubborn, slow, suspicious, ignorant and passionate'. Maria della Robbia, who was farming in Chianti in the 1920s, tells a wonderful story about her efforts to persuade her *contadini* to tell the truth (not, it seems, part of their culture). Her *fattora* had agreed a selling price with a neighbour for a cow. Signora della Robbia insisted he tell the neighbour that the cow was a poor milker. 'But *signora*, we will not get the good price we have agreed!' The *signora* insisted. After the sale the *fattora* returned triumphant. He had got the full price, even though he had told the truth. The buyer had assumed the *fattora* was lying, that the cow was so good the seller had got a better offer, so he insisted the deal be done as agreed.

25 FROM PITIGLIANO TO SOVANA

See also photograph pages 12-13

Distance/time: 6km/3.8mi; 1h35min (12km/7.6mi; 3h10min return)

Grade: moderate, with an ascent of 70m/230ft. You must be sure-footed; there is a bit of scrambling on all fours where the path is steep and rocky. Suitable all year round, but *not* after heavy rain.

Equipment: as pages 137-138; also walking boots

How to get there: RAMA 🚌 from Grosseto to Pitigliano; journey time 2h. Or 🚗: park at Pitigliano (the 100km-point in Car tour 8) if you are returning by bus; park at either Pitigliano or Sovana (the 45km-point in Car tour 8) if you are walking out and back; the route is easy to find in either direction, as it bears red and white waymarks.

To return: occasional RAMA 🚌 *(weekdays only; enquire in advance),* from Sovana to Pitigliano; journey time 10min

Refreshments: bar/restaurants at Pitigliano and Sovana

Full of interest, this walk links a medieval town packed tight above a vertical cliff to a miniature medieval village full of charm and historic buildings. The route is through an area rich in Etruscan remains — tombs, temples, and drainage channels cut into the rock. Much of the walk is along their sunken roads, worn deep into the terrain through the pressure of wheels and hooves on soft volcanic rock. When the ruts became too deep, the humps in the middle were chiselled away, so the roads got deeper and deeper. Some roads are as much as 10m/30ft deep, although these were probably cut for ceremonial purposes rather than eroded. These deep roads are shady and cool. As the whole walk traverses quiet landscapes rich in wild flowers, it is definitely a five-star hike!

Start the walk in the main square (PIAZZA REPUBBLICA) in **Pitigliano**. Via Roma and Via Zuccarelli are streets that lead together off the square. Take VIA ZUCCARELLI, to penetrate the town's enchanting *centro storico,* with its labyrinth of narrow alleys. The alleys off to the left lead to the vertical drop that marks the end of the town (photograph pages 12-13). When you meet VIA ALDOBRANDESCHI, turn left to descend gently down the spine of the town. Almost at the end you will see a gate, the PORTA DI SOVANA (**10min**), down steps to the right. Leave the town through this gate; you immediately meet a junction of tracks. Choose the one directly ahead, veering to the left, the red- and white-waymarked VIA CAVA POGGIO CANI (not named, however, until you get to the bottom of the hill). Descend on this track, cut into the volcanic tufa. If this is your first experience of an Etruscan sunken road, you are sure to be impressed by their antiquity and air of mystery. This one meets a village 'street' of rock-hewn caves. Just *before* these caves, turn right at a Y-FORK.

At the ROAD (**20min**), turn right to cross the **River Lente** on a bridge. Ignore the track immediately to the left, but carry on for a few strides, until you see a path off to the left diving

130

THE ETRUSCANS

There seems to be an air of mystery about these ancient people, perhaps because most of what we know about them comes from their necropolises or 'cities of the dead'.

They lived in an area of Italy surrounded by the rivers Arno and Tiber and the Tyrennian Sea, from the ninth to the first centuries before Christ. It is not surprising then that much physical evidence of their way of life has been annihilated by successive civilisations — with the exception of their burial sites.

The Etruscans believed that to have worldly belongings with them in their tomb would help their passage to the next life. To the great delight of archaeologists (and grave-robbers), the tombs were therefore filled with these necessities. Not only that, many of the stone coffins were carved with realistic scenes from mythology and daily life, then topped with a likeness of the occupant. The tombs were sited outside the towns, often in the valleys by rivers. They varied greatly in shape and size — some like rooms, some like temples, some circular with columns. Part of the terrain occupied by the Etruscans was tufa, rock rather similar to pumice. It is a soft rock, perfect for excavating tomb-caves.

The Etruscans were great traders and sailors in the Mediterranean area and beyond. As they travelled they collected ideas and artefacts to enrich their own culture. A visit to a museum devoted to the Etruscans will give you an insight into the sophistication of their life-style.

They were also experts in mining, intensive agriculture, land reclamation, metal-working, pottery, art and sculpture, even dentistry.

They seem also to be a people who enjoyed the good things in life. War and expanding their empire were not priorities. Inevitably, some may say, this civilisation did not survive. After several disastrous defeats from 535BC onwards, they were unable to withstand the advancing Romans. In 395BC Rome captured Veii, which signalled the end of Etruscan independence. By 90BC the Etruscan people were granted Roman citizenship.

Typical Etruscan sunken road

up and into the cliff. This is Via Cava dell'Annunziata, another extraordinary trail that curls and zigzags its way uphill. Ignore all but the main clear track cut into the rock. Inevitably, as the rock is so soft and the way so old, there are places where you will need to climb over debris, but there is nothing too daunting. It is a steep climb, but so fascinating you'll hardly notice. Once at the top (**40min**), take the unsealed road to the right.

Very soon the road divides by a farm: fork left, then go left again almost immediately, along a track crossing farmland. Where the track sweeps round through some imposing gate-posts, leave it to go through a less-grand wooden gate. You cross a scrubby plateau, where broom and ilex trees eke out an existence on almost-bare rock, rutted by the passage of cart wheels over hundreds of years. The route generally follows the ruts, but is also well waymarked as it heads northwest towards Sovana's distant cathedral. After running alongside a fence, the trail descends to cross a stream, alongside the remains of the old stone bridge shown opposite (bottom). You emerge at a field (**1h10min**) — a sunny, sheltered picnic spot, even in winter. Walk left across the field, then take a track heading up to the left. This too is a deeply-rutted sunken road (photograph page 131); the central channel can make walking difficult and slippery, so it needs some concentration.

At the end of this 'road' take the track to the left. Join the road to Sovana and turn right. After crossing the river, the road climbs to the ruined castle. Take the road at the left of the castle and follow it to the main street of **Sovana** (**1h 35min**), with its tiny town hall, cathedral and restaurants. The bus stop is in the main street, by the petrol station. If no bus is due, walk back to Pitigliano the way you came.

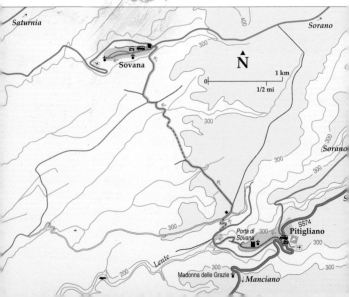

WILD FOOD

Free food was very important to the country people. The knowledge of which plants are edible has been handed down from generation to generation. The people doing the original research were probably peasants driven to the edge of starvation by calamities such as epidemics, which severely disrupted food supplies. Folk historians describe the skill of the peasants in making even poisonous plants edible.

One historian, Piero Camporesi, believes that hungry peasants added narcotic seeds to their bread to make their hard lives bearable. Collecting wild food is a habit deeply rooted in the old country people. Even today you can see them setting off on their *passeggiata*, with a plastic bag and a small knife in one hand — just in case they see something edible along the way.

My Italian book of edible wild plants lists 316 varieties to collect and eat. There are the wild versions of the foods and herbs we already know — onions, garlic, asparagus, marjoram, thyme, bay and fennel. For the most part, however, it lists numerous wild plants with leaves that are eaten when picked young — in salads, soups or risottos. These include mallow, daisy, dandelion, toadflax, lesser celandine, and many others.

Fungi are the most important wild food still collected today, with their accompanying fatalities. Chemists' shops in Italy do provide an indentification service, and this is vital, as some types of fungus are so toxic that even to put them in your basket can be lethal!

Some common wild foods are listed below, but you may also like to try *Crostini alla calendula*. Pick the tender young petals of the marigold *(Calendula officinalis)*, common from March to June. Add them to mayonnaise and spread on olive-oiled toast. Decorate with a flower!

Wild hops: This is a hedgerow plant that likes to be near water. Just the tender top leaves and shoots are eaten, boiled with garlic or added to risotto or soup. Small quantities can be added to salads.

Asparagus: It is easier to see wild asparagus *after* its 'eat-by date'. The long ferny fronds are recognisable as being part of the foliage with flowers from the florist. But it is the young shoots which must be collected, just after they pop up from

Aqueduct at Pitigliano (top); cart ruts on the plateau; old stone bridge with CAI waymarks (1h10min)

the soil. This is usually at the end of March and April. The new shoots are hidden in shady hedgerows. You cook them as you cook cultivated asparagus, although for a much *continued on page 135*

26 CIRCUIT FROM SATURNIA

See photograph page 39   **Distance/time:** 18km/11mi; 5h

Grade: easy, with a total ascent of 300m/1000ft; little shade

Equipment: as pages 137-138; also swimming things and waterproof boots in winter (river to ford)

How to get there and return: Rama 🚌 from Grosseto to/from Saturnia (only *one bus a day,* in the afternoon); journey time 2h. Or 🚗: park in the village square at Saturnia (the 70km-point on Car tour 8)

Refreshments: bars and restaurants in Saturnia

Short walk: Saturnia — Terme di Saturnia — Saturnia (4.5km/3mi; 1h). Easy, with an ascent of only 140m/460ft; equipment as pages 137-138, plus bathing things. Follow the main walk to the 50min-point, then continue straight back into Saturnia.

This is the most relaxing of walks — perhaps meander is a better description. There are no real hills to climb, no navigation problems, no traffic or people. You can even take a thermal bath along the way, either in the little hot stream coming from the hotel complex or in a hot waterfall (I recommend the latter — it's like a natural sauna). The gentle undulating hills are covered with cereal crops, pastures and woodlands which makes a varied patchwork. In June the

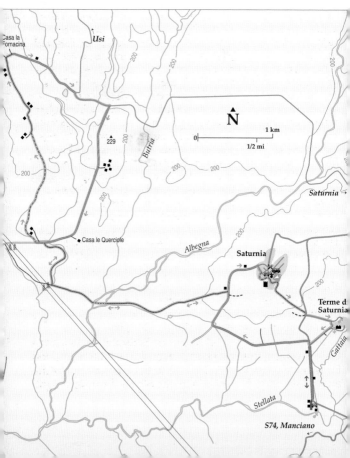

Out for a walk, ready to collect wild food; Capparis spinosa (top left); fungi in a basket

shorter time. The wild variety is said to taste infinitely better.

Oregano: This evocative Italian herb is common in gardens and in the wild. Several varieties are cultivated, but in the wild it is *Origanum vulgare* you are likely to find growing on dry scrubby areas and sunny banks. It is prized for its many uses in the kitchen, the pharmacy and to scent the house. It is also an ancient symbol of happiness, so was made into wreaths for newly-married couples to wear.

Thyme: It is always easy to test whether you have found the right herb: just rub its leaves between your fingers and smell. Thyme is not difficult to recognise, with its tiny leaves growing from short woody stems and its profusion of pink flowers in summer. Like its sister herb, oregano, it flourishes in dry rocky soils, often seeming to transform them into rock gardens. Its essential oil has many uses in herbal medicine.

Capers (Capparis spinosa): These splendid plants cascade down from walls, decorating them with delicate flowers of white petals with a mass of pink stamens. As usual, in Tuscany these plants are used for more than decoration. The flower buds are edible. The buds are raked off and pickled or preserved in salt. They are used to add piquancy to savoury food. The pickled fruit are edible too, but you see them less often. The buds are eaten on pizzas in some countries, but not in Italy.

Wild plum (Sloe): In March and April the rough hilltops are covered with clouds of white blossom. This is the flower of the spiny wild plum. As it grows more like a shrub than a tree, it is not a friend to walkers, often blocking an ill-used path with a dense mass of spiny branches. But we forgive it, as its blossoms are so ethereal, and its fruit such an intense musky-blue. These wild plums are edible when cooked (the raw fruit is too bitter). Added to plenty of sugar, they make a delicious jam or jelly; added to alcohol they make a delicately-flavoured drink, such as sloe gin. The leaves can be brewed into a tea and the flowers infused to soothe coughs. And the wood, which is very hard, was used to make farm implements and walking sticks.

abundance of nature is overwhelming: hedgerows and verges more luxuriant with flowers than many gardens, butterflies you may have only ever seen in books, and a cacophony of birdsong and chirping insects.

Start the walk in the village of **Saturnia** on Via della Chiesa: walk in front of the church and down the signposted Etruscan 'Clodia Road'. This stone track passes under the arch of the Porta Romana. With the old castle on your right, follow this CAI-waymarked trail to the junction with the main road. Cross the road and follow the signs to the 'TERME'. Just before the HOTEL COMPLEX (**15min**), take the road to the right, along the edge of the TENNIS COURTS. (Beyond the car park here, a grassy track on the left leads to the small warm-water river, where people bathe.) Continue along the tree-lined road until you reach the main road again. (If you would like to explore the hot waterfalls shown on page 39, take a 10-minute diversion here: turn left along the road, go past the petrol station and, at the bend in the road, take a track to the right — in front of a well-hidden bar and restaurant. The track leads to the falls.)

Cross the main road, walk a short way to the right, then take an unsealed road on the left (signposted to houses 195/187; **20min**). This road circles below Saturnia. Ignore the next road on the right, but take the following right turn (at a T-JUNCTION; **40min**). This stony track climbs up the hill back to Saturnia. When you come to a waymarked track just before a house (**50min**), turn left. *(But continue straight ahead for the Short walk.)* With vineyards in the foreground and spreading hills and rivers in the distance, you descend to the river, where the vegetation becomes wilder and the flowers more glorious. The river bed is dry in the summer, just a mass of smooth rocks. Keep to the main track, veering left. It leads to a short CONCRETE FORD across the **Albegna River** (**1h20min**).

Keep to the waymarked track, passing fields of cereals, until you cross a second river on a concrete bridge (**1h 30min**). A grassy track now takes you through the field on the right. After closing the gate carefully, follow the track beside the river to an UNSEALED ROAD (**1h45min**). Turn left and pass by an archetypal Tuscan farmhouse on a little knoll. After the entrance to the farm, turn right through a wire gate, into a field. Follow the waymarked path straight ahead, along the edges of fields, to another FARM (**2h20min**) with prickly pear growing up the barn wall. Continue straight on past two houses, with a view of the valley to the left, then past huge, centuries-old olive trees.

You now meet the FIRST OF FOUR JUNCTIONS (**2h55min**) which come up in the next 20 minutes. Keep right at all of them. (If you cross the Butria River on a high road bridge, you have gone too far.) After the FOURTH JUNCTION (**3h15min**), you should be walking up a rough, partly-tarmacked road that leads back towards the pretty farmhouse on the knoll. Within sight of the farm, take the river track again, just across the BRIDGE (**3h45min**). Turn left here, to retrace your steps via the FORD over the river bed. When you have reached the top of the lane, turn left at the T-JUNCTION by the house, back to **Saturnia** (**5h**).

Hints for walkers

When to walk in Tuscany

Tuscany is a wonderful place for walkers, as its temperate climate and geography make it possible to walk there all year round. The myth of continuous sunshine is not totally baseless. The winter can produce many gloriously sunny days, perfect for walking. But late spring, especially May, is probably the best time of year, followed by autumn.

There are two snags to bear in mind. Tuscany's weather is unpredictable; there can be snow at Easter, cool temperatures in August, or a week of rain in June. The weather can also be extreme, with long periods of very heavy rain (especially in October and November), and extremes of temperature in the winter and summer. As with so much in Italy, the secret is to be flexible and well prepared. Fortunately there are plenty of museums and churches to visit, if being out-of-doors is not an option.

July and August have the most predictable weather: it is hot, sometimes *very hot;* thus they are the least suitable months for walking. But by starting early in the morning, it *is* still possible to walk — in wooded mountain areas.

Walking in the mountains needs special care. Check the local weather forecasts, or talk with the local people. In winter, walking in the mountains of Tuscany is a completely different sport, needing proper equipment, expertise and local knowledge. Unexpected storms are common, especially in the spring and autumn.

Where to stay

For those relying on public transport, it is better to stay in a city, probably either Florence (Firenze) or Siena. If you have a car, you can choose a more rural setting. For mountain lovers, staying towards the north of Tuscany would be more convenient.

We always stay at farms that rent rooms or apartments. They are usually in the prettiest places (see photograph pages 34-35, of a high standard and not expensive. You can get information from tourist offices, newsagents' catalogues, or on the internet at: www.agriturismo.regione.toscana.it

What to wear

In warm, dry weather, I recommend light cotton clothes, usually long trousers and a long-sleeved shirt over a T-shirt. This is for protection from sun, brambles and insects. If you may be walking in hot sun, *protection is essential:* sunhat, sunglasses and a high-factor sun cream.

Trainers or strong shoes with good grip are fine for all the walks, except where walking boots are specified. But wearing modern hiking boots is not a hardship: they are very lightweight and they give welcome ankle support and grip. Do *not* wear sandals: they give no protection from snakes.

For wintry weather, wear your clothing in layers, so that you can make adjustments as your body temperature changes. Avoid denim jeans, as they can be very cold, especially if they get wet. *Whatever* the weather, at the start of a winter's day, I *always* pack gloves, scarf, hat and· a windproof, waterproof jacket and trousers.

What to carry

For very short walks, you really need nothing except perhaps your camera and a bottle of water in the summer. But most of the walks are long enough to demand a few essentials.

In summer you *must take plenty to drink* (at least 2 litres for a whole day's walk). Many Italians bottle water from wayside springs for home consumption. Ask the locals whether it is safe to drink: 'E pot**a**bile, l'acqua?' or use purifying tablets if want to be sure. Take sun protection as mentioned above, and insect repellent.

In winter, as well as extra clothing and waterproofs, I pack extra food and a torch carried in a waterproof rucksack.

For walks in wilder areas, as well as the above take a compass, perhaps an area map (see page 40), a whistle, and matches. A stick can be really useful; it lessens the wear on your knees, and gives wonderful support for obstacles such as fords, tricky ascents and for passing big dogs!

Whenever you walk, always carry a small first aid kit, a knife, and some high-energy food, like sweets or dried fruit.

What you *need* to know

There are no dangers in Tuscany that you won't find in any other western country: cars, dogs, insects, and people! Don't let any of the following put you off. To be forewarned is to be forearmed.

There are poisonous **snakes**: vipers, which are brownish-grey, with a diamond-shaped head. They are very timid and only bite if they feel threatened. Take care where you put your hands and feet, *and do not walk in sandals*. Bites are rare, as are deaths caused by bites. If you were to be bitten, keep calm, bind the limb firmly, and get to help as quickly as possible. Some Italian trekkers buy a snake bite kit *(siero antivipera)* from the chemist and carry it with them.

Guard **dogs** close to houses are very noisy, especially as your passing is probably the only excitement of their day. I have found them generally to be firmly tied up, so I just keep walking. Carrying a stick or a Dog Dazer (available from Sunflower Books) is a good idea if you are nervous.

Ticks live in the grass in the Tuscan hills, waiting to attach themselves to the skin of any passing creature. Keep your skin covered and check your skin after a walk in the mountains. The clothing I recommend will lessen your exposure.

The **hunting season** (see article page 76) is September to March, although it can be shorter. If you walk in the autumn, you will hear the sound of gun-fire. Talk loudly, to let the hunters know you are coming, and *stay on the path*. Hunters are generally polite, cautious and helpful.

How to ask for help

Near the towns you will find people know some English and like to practice it, especially young people. In the country, people are very keen to help, but you will have to ask them in Italian. (Showing country people a map is not usually much use.) It helps to ask directions in such a way that the answer is Yes or No. For example, ask a key question ('Where is the road to …?'), then follow it up quickly with a secondary question needing a yes/no answer ('Is it straight ahead?').

Key questions

English	Italian	Approximate pronunciation
English	*Italian*	*Approximate pronunciation*
Good day —	Buon giorno —	Bwon **jor**no
Hello —	Salve —	**Sal**vay
I am lost.	Mi sono perso.	Mee **soh**noh **payr**so.
Where is	Dov'è	Do**vay**
the road to …?	la strada per …?	la **strah**da payr
the path to …?	il sentiero per …?	il **saynt**yero payr
the bus stop?	la fermata?	la fayr**mah**ta
Goodbye.	Arrivederci.	Arreevay**dayr**chee.

Secondary question, leading to a yes/no

Is it here?/there!	E qua?/là	E **qua**?/**la**?
straight ahead?	a diritto?	a dee**reet**to?
behind?	dietro?	a dee**ay**tro?
to the left?	a sinistra?	a seenee**es**tra?
to the right?	a destra?	a **des**tra?
above?/below?	sopra?/sotto?	**soh**pra?/**soht**to?
up?/down?	su?/giù?	**soo**?/**joo**?
near?	vicino?	vee**chee**no?

Other useful words and phrases

Mr/Mrs	Signore/Signora	Seen**yoh**ray/Seen**yoh**ra
first/second	primo/secondo	**pree**mo/se**con**do
We are going to …	Andiamo a …	Andi**a**mo a
Please —	Per favore —	Payr fa**voh**ray
Show us	Ci può indicare	Chee pwo indi**car**ay
the way	la strada	la **strah**da
Thank you.	Grazie.	**Grats**yay.

People in Tuscany usually say hello when they pass you along a country lane and when they go into a bar or shop. I hope you will respond in a similarly friendly manner.

B uses

While almost all of the walks in this book are most easily reached by car, you should also be able to reach the majority by bus (or train). But remember that on Sundays public transport is less frequent. Although you will be able to obtain timetables for many buses from the larger tourist offices, the safest option is to visit the bus company itself. Below is a list of all the operators serving the routes to and from the walks.

Buses from Florence

All of the following companies have their termini, information offices and ticket offices around Piazza di Stazione in central Florence.

ATAF — for the city and suburbs
Terminus at Piazza di Stazione
tel: 055 5650222

SITA — for the south (Chianti), north, and eastern regions
Terminus at Via S Caterina da Siena
tel: 800 373760

CAP — for the north (Mugello)
Terminus at Largo Alinari 9
tel: 055 214637

LAZZI — for the Arno Valley, Pisa, Lucca, and the northern coast
Terminus at Piazza Adua
tel: 055 351061

Buses from Siena

TRA-IN — for the city and region
Local terminus at Piazza A. Gramsci
tel: 0577 204246
Regional terminus at Piazza San Domenico
tel: 0577 204245,
'Prontorario' — instant timetable
tel: 0577 204270

Buses from Lucca

CLAP — for the Garfagnana and the northern coast
Terminus at Piazza Verdi
tel: 0583 587897

LAZZI — for Pisa, Florence and the northern coast
Terminus at Piazza Verdi
tel: 0583 584876

Buses from Pietrasanta

CLAP — for the Alpi Apuane
Terminus at Piazzale G Castagna, by the railway station
tel: 0584 792107

Buses from Grosseto

RAMA — for southern Tuscany
Terminus at Piazza Marconi, by the railway station
tel: 0564 6425215

Useful words for reading the timetables are: *giornale:* daily, *feriale:* Mondays to Fridays and/or Saturdays; *festivo:* Sundays and holidays.

You must have a ticket before you board the bus. Buy them at the bus stations and at bars displaying the company logos. When you board the bus you must then **validate** the ticket by stamping it in the machine by the 'in' door. Buy your return ticket with your outward journey ticket.

Bus stops display the name of the company and the word FERMATA (bus stop).

Refreshments

Preparing for picnics is easy, as there are delicatessen counters in supermarkets and grocers *(alimentari)*. These are filled with cooked meats, *prosciutto crudo* or *cotto* (raw or cooked ham), salamis and cheeses of all sorts, especially sheep cheese *(pecorino)*. Some wonderful meat-and-fruit combinations are pear and *pecorino, finocchio* (a fennel-flavoured salami) and figs, *prociutto crudo* and melon.

Tuscan bread must be bought fresh every day, as it goes hard very quickly. It is made without salt, so improves with tasty accompaniments, such as olives. *Schiacciata,* a flat bread covered in oil and salt makes great sandwiches. Bars sell sandwiches *(panini)* to take away, sometimes cut to order. They can be two door-steps of Tuscan bread with a slice of something between — good but rather dry. I always pack fruit and salad to add a little moisture. Semi-dried fruit is great for providing natural sugar, and nuts for protein.

Bars, trattorias and restaurants generally provide consistently good fresh food at a reasonable price. Choosing local dishes is usually a good bet. Where an eating place is mentioned by name, it is because I have tried it. Remember that many places, restaurants and food shops, are closed Mondays. It is good always to pack a little something, just in case.

The country code and safety guidelines

It is important that Tuscany is no worse off for you (or me) having visited. A wonderful maxim is 'Take only photographs, leave only foot-prints'. These simple guidelines are obvious, but important:

- **Only light fires** at picnic places with fireplaces.
- **Don't frighten animals.**
- **Walk quietly** through farms, and take care not to provoke the dogs.
- **Leave gates as you find them.**
- **Protect all wild and cultivated plants.** *Never* walk over cultivated land.
- **Take all litter away with you.**

- **Be friendly and polite.**
- **For your own safety:**
  — Don't attempt walks beyond your capacity. Check the guidelines on grade and equipment, taking care not to overestimate your energy.
  — Stay on the path.
  — Do not wander off the described route if there is any sign of mist or if it is late in the day.
  — **Never walk alone in remote areas.**
  — Always tell a responsible person exactly where you are going and when you expect to return.
  — Be properly equipped (see notes on page 138).
  — Check the local weather forecast before you set off, if you are going into the mountains. Some mountain walks will not be possible in the winter.
  — At any time the walk may become unsafe, perhaps because of a landslide after heavy rain. If the route is not as described in this book, and the way ahead is not secure, do not attempt to continue.
  — Read the **'Important note'** on page 2.
  — **Do not take risks! This is the most important point of all.**

Emergency telephone numbers
All these are 24-hour services. The equivalent of 999 in the UK is 113, and is only to be used in grave emergencies or when you cannot contact the appropriate service directly.
Carabinieri (police) *and* alpine rescue: 112
Fire: 115
Ambulance: 118

Index

Geographical names comprise the only entries in this index; for non-geographical subjects see Contents, page 3. A page number in _italic type_ refers to a map; **bold type** refers to a photograph. Both of these may be in addition to a text reference on the same page. Pronunciation guide: where a syllable in a place name is in **bold**, stress that syllable. Otherwise stress the next to the last syllable (e.g. A**zza**no).

143